MW00581117

# MEASURES *of* SUCCESS®

## A Comprehensive Musicianship Band Method

DEBORAH A. SHELDON • BRIAN BALMAGES • TIMOTHY LOEST • ROBERT SHELDON

PERCUSSION WRITTEN AND EDITED BY DAVID COLLIER

Congratulations on completing the first book of *Measures of Success,* and welcome to Book 2! Throughout this book, you will explore music from many different countries around the world and learn about many composers that you did not encounter in Book 1. You will also explore some of the fascinating historical events and literature that help bring the days of these composers to life.

This book includes 2 accompaniment CDs that contain performance tracks with live musicians playing the music from your book, as well as accompaniment tracks so you can play along. Additional CDs that cover the remainder of the book can be purchased at your local music dealer or downloaded at www.fjhmusic.com/mos.

Enjoy this exciting time in your musical growth. As you practice, you will continue to find yourself sharing the gift of music with family, friends, and audiences.

Ready?

Let's make music!

## ABOUT THIS BOOK

Similar to Book 1, this book is divided into two main sections. The first section includes snare drum, bass drum, accessory percussion and timpani. These pages are often divided into A and B pages because there are multiple instruments you will learn. The second section contains all of the keyboard percussion exercises. Be sure to work from both sides of the book so that you become a *complete percussionist!* Finally, look at the last page of the book for a list of **recommended sticks and mallets.**

Production: Frank J. Hackinson
Production Coordinators: Ken Mattis and Brian Balmages
Cover Design and Interior Line Drawings: Danielle Taylor and Adrianne Hirosky
Interior Layout and Design: Andi Whitmer
Engraving: Tempo Music Press, Inc.
Printer: Tempo Music Press, Inc.

THE FJH MUSIC COMPANY INC.
Frank J. Hackinson

ISBN-13: 978-1-56939-901-9

# PRELUDE: THE WARM-UP

The **warm-up** prepares you for individual practice or rehearsal. Much as an athlete warms up before an event, musicians must do the same thing. Play these exercises with and without the CD each time you practice.

## 1. STEADY AS SHE GOES

## 2. SOUND BUILDER

## 3. HALF AND HALF

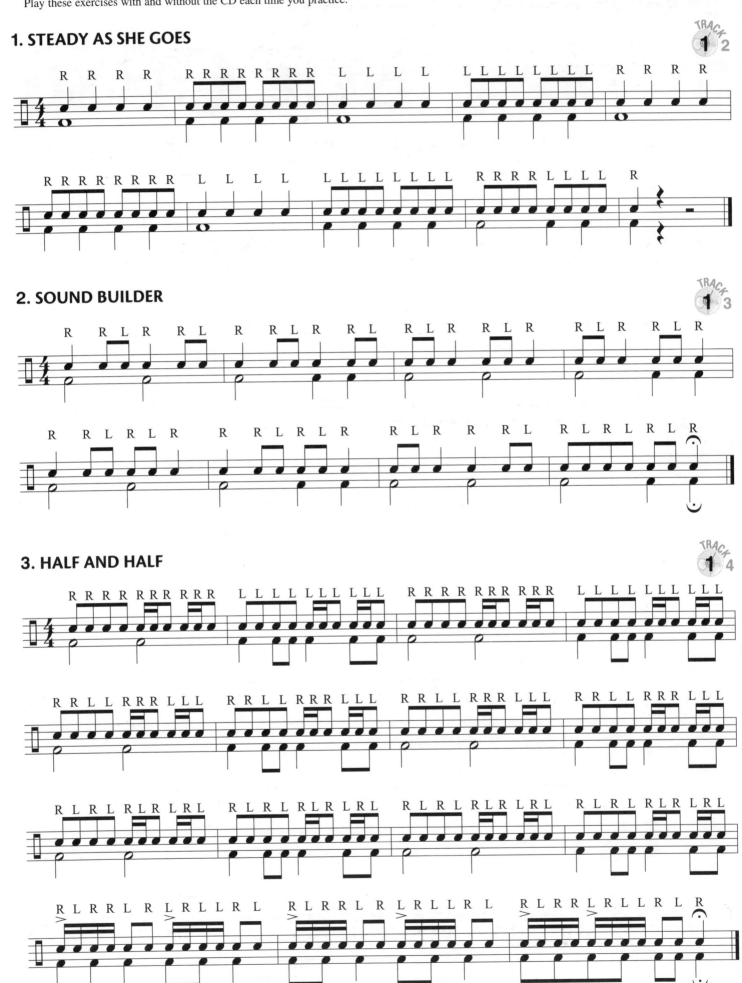

## 4. CHORALE – Trio or Full Band
*For multiple bounce rolls with fermatas,
lift off the drum at the release and do not play a tap.*

## 5. CHORALE (BEFIEHL DU DEINE WEGE) – Full Band

J.S. Bach

# ✦ OPUS 1: RECAPITULATION

A **recapitulation** is a summary that restates the main points of a subject. In music, a recapitulation occurs after a development section and presents the main themes of a movement for a final time. Your musicianship developed substantially in Book 1, so the following recapitulation will reacquaint you with many of the concepts you have already learned.

## LET'S REVIEW

The following music will help you to remember these important elements:

## 1.1 GIVE ME FIVE!

**TRACK 1 / 7**

## 1.2 SUR LE PONT D'AVIGNON  *Focus on connecting multiple bounce strokes on eighth notes.*

French Folk Song  **TRACK 1 / 8**

## 1.3 THIS OLD MAN

English Folk Song

## 1.4 ORANGES AND LEMONS

English Folk Song

## 1.5 THEME FROM SONATA NO. 11

Wolfgang Amadeus Mozart

4a

The following music will help you to remember these important elements:

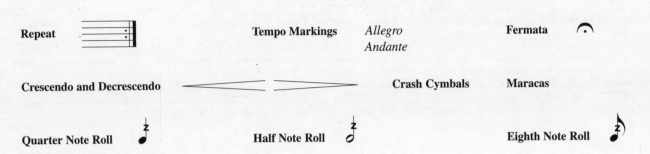

## 1.6 FADING FANFARE

TRACK 1 12

FOR PERCUSSION ONLY – Snare Drum Roll Exercises

**1.7 AURA LEE** *Focus on an even sound as you play quarter and half note rolls.*

American Folk Song — TRACK 1/13

**1.8 LOS POLLITOS**

**Allegro**

Mexican Folk Song — TRACK 1/14

## HISTORY

### MUSIC

Polish composer **Frédéric Chopin** (1810–1845), much like Mozart, was a musical prodigy who began composing at a very early age. He was an accomplished pianist and all of his works involve the piano. His *Fantaisie-Impromptu* is one of his best-known pieces, despite the fact he never wanted it to be published!

### LITERATURE

In 1834, when *Fantaisie-Impromptu* was written, the great Russian poet and author Alexander Pushkin wrote the short story *The Queen of Spades,* a tale of human greed. Composers Tchaikovsky and Franz von Suppé both wrote operas based on Pushkin's story.

### WORLD

In 1834, final modifications were made to the present form of Braille, a system used to help the blind read and write. Fish lovers sent up a cheer when sardines were canned for the first time in Europe.

**1.9 FANTAISIE-IMPROMPTU**

**Andante**

Frédéric Chopin — TRACK 1/15

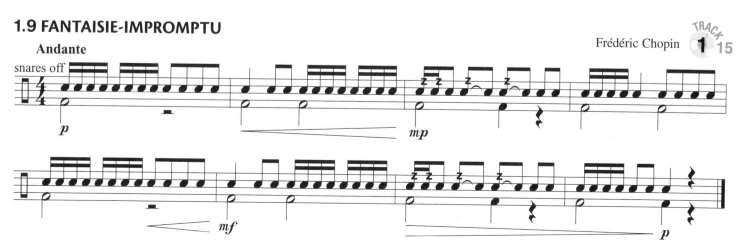

5a

## LET'S REVIEW

The following music will help you to remember these important elements:

| Time Signature | **2/4** | Eighth Rest | ⅞ | Timpani |
| Tempo Marking | *Moderato* | Pick-up Note | | Tambourine |
| Dotted Quarter Note Rolls | | Flamacue | | |

### 1.10 THEME FROM SYMPHONY NO. 1 – Duet
Johannes Brahms    TRACK 1 16

### 1.10 THEME FROM SYMPHONY NO. 1 – Timpani
Johannes Brahms    TRACK 1 16

### 1.11 ALL NIGHT, ALL DAY
Traditional Spiritual    TRACK 1 17

5b

 **HISTORY**

## MUSIC

**Jacques Offenbach** (1819–1880) was born in Germany as "Jacob" but became "Jacques" when he moved to Paris to study cello at the Paris Conservatoire. He is best known for his operettas (he wrote almost 100 of them!), including *Orpheus in the Underworld,* which includes the famous *Can-can.*

## LITERATURE

Henry Wadsworth Longfellow wrote the narrative poem *The Courtship of Miles Standish.* Standish was a passenger on the Mayflower and became Plymouth Colony's assistant governor. Just a few years later, Charles Dickens wrote *Great Expectations,* a story of an orphan boy named Pip who faced personal struggles that shaped his life and character.

## WORLD

In 1858, a series of seven debates between Abraham Lincoln and Stephen Douglas were held in Illinois. That year, Minnesota was admitted to the union as the 32$^{nd}$ state. Pencils with attached erasers, as well as rotary washing machines, were patented.

### 1.12 CAN-CAN

Jacques Offenbach

**TRACK 1 18**

**Allegro**

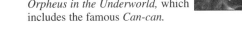
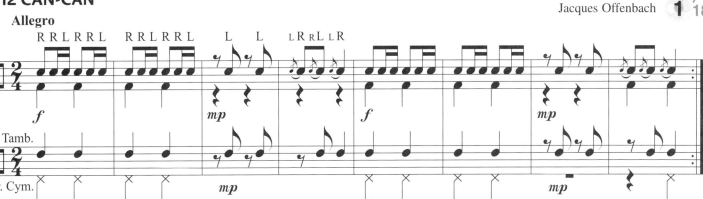

### 1.13 CRIPPLE CREEK

Appalachian Folk Song

**TRACK 1 19**

**Brightly**

---

✳ **FOR PERCUSSION ONLY**

These exercises focus on dotted quarter note rolls.

### 1.14 THE MARINES' HYMN

Official Song of the U.S. Marine Corps

**TRACK 1 20**

**March tempo**

## LET'S REVIEW

The following music will help you to remember these important elements:

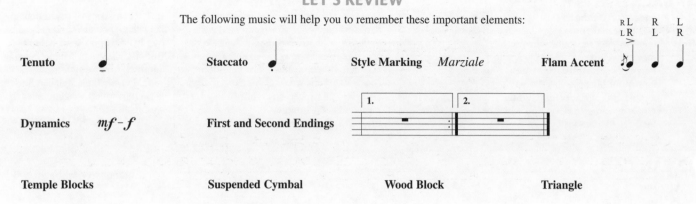

Tenuto

Staccato

Style Marking   *Marziale*

Flam Accent

Dynamics   *mf - f*

First and Second Endings

Temple Blocks

Suspended Cymbal

Wood Block

Triangle

## 1.15 THE MAN ON THE FLYING TRAPEZE

Gaston Lyle

## 1.16 THE CUCKOO WOODPECKER

## 1.17 BACKYARD STOMP

## 1.18 TURKISH MARCH

Wolfgang Amadeus Mozart

## 1.19 FLOWER DRUM SONG

Chinese Folk Song

## 1.20 TECHNIQUE TWISTER

7a

## LET'S REVIEW

The following music will help you to remember these important elements:    **Claves**

### 1.21 CHA-CHA CHROMATICA

### 1.22 TWO-FACED POLKA

### HISTORY

**MUSIC**

*Hungarian Dance No. 5* comes from a set of 21 dances written by **Johannes Brahms** (1833–1897) and based mostly on Hungarian melodies. Ironically, Brahms accidentally based this piece on a folk dance by another composer, Kéler Béla, thinking that it was a traditional folk song.

**LITERATURE**

Leo Tolstoy wrote his epic novel *War and Peace,* a work of historical fiction that is considered a classic to this day. American novelist Louisa May Alcott, who is best known for writing *Little Women,* published the sequel entitled *Good Wives,* which followed the lives of the *Little Women* as they grew into adulthood.

**WORLD**

In 1869, the Suez Canal opened in Egypt. This man-made waterway connects the Mediterranean and Red Seas. John Willis Menard became the first African-American to speak in Congress in that same year. The Cincinnati Red Stockings became the first professional baseball team in the United States.

### 1.23 HUNGARIAN DANCE NO. 5

Johannes Brahms

# 1.24 FINGER TWISTER

# 1.24a IT'S ABOUT TIME – Snare Drum Solo

David Collier

# OPUS 1 ENCORE!

## INTERPRETATION STATION

Listen to CD 1 Track 31. You will hear two versions of each example.
Choose the version (A or B) that has better phrasing. Circle your answer.

1. A  B        2. A  B        3. A  B        4. A  B

## SIMON "SEZ"

Listen to CD 1 Track 32. You will hear a well-known musical work. Listen first, sing it, then find the pitches on your keyboard percussion instrument. You can then play along with the accompaniment track that follows. Can you match the notes and style of the recording?

## COMPOSER'S CORNER

Complete this composition. Refer to the time signature. Remember to add dynamics.
Give your piece a title and perform it for a friend or family member!

Title:_____  Name:_____

## PENCIL POWER

In Opus 1, you reviewed many of the musical concepts you learned in *Measures of Success* Book 1.
Match each item on the left with its correct term or definition by writing in the appropriate letter.

1. _____ *Marziale*
2. _____ ⅞
3. _____
4. _____ *Andante*
5. _____
6. _____ *Allegro*
7. _____ *rit.*
8. _____ 2/4
9. _____
10. _____
11. _____
12. _____
13. _____
14. _____
15. _____
16. _____

A. Paradiddle
B. Walking Tempo
C. Fast Tempo
D. Gradually Slow Down
E. Accent
F. Gradually Get Louder
G. Fermata
H. Repeat
I. Flam
J. Double Paradiddle
K. Flamacue
L. Eighth Rest
M. March Style
N. Eighth Note Roll
O. Flam Tap
P. Time Signature

BB210PER

## CURTAIN UP!

Time to perform! Play this piece for friends or family members. Remember to introduce the piece by its title and bow when you are finished.

### 1.25 CHESTER

William Billings

### 1.25 CHESTER – Timpani

William Billings

# ✳ OPUS 2

## 2.1 SEPARATION ANXIETY

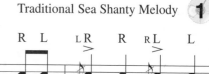

## 2.2 THE GRUMPY PIRATE *Notice the flam accents in measures 1, 3, 5 and 7.*

Traditional Sea Shanty Melody

**Animato** *(animated or lively)*

## BONGOS

**Bongos** are a set of two small wooden-shelled drums that are approximately 7 and 8 inches in diameter and are attached. They originated in Cuba with African influences. These drums often have thick calfskin heads and are played with fingers or thin sticks. For right-handed players, the small drum is on the left and the large drum is on the right.

### ✳ FOR PERCUSSION ONLY

*Focus on a consistent, even sound.*

**A**

*Isolate each two-measure phrase. When you are ready, play the entire exercise without stopping.*

**B**

**2.3 RUMBA CUBANA!** *A rumba is a rhythmic Cuban dance that has Spanish and African origins.*

**CONDUCTING REVIEW: 4/4 TIME**

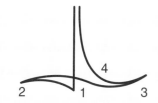

**2.4 CHICKEN ON A FENCE POST**

American Folk Song

BB210PER

10a

| HISTORY | MUSIC | LITERATURE | WORLD |
|---|---|---|---|
| | **George M. Cohan** (1878–1942), known as "Mr. Broadway", wrote many musicals that were staged on Broadway in New York. His memorable melodies are still loved and sung today. Some of his most notable songs are *Yankee Doodle Dandy, Give My Regards to Broadway,* and *You're a Grand Old Flag,* a song that paid tribute to the U.S. flag and won him a Congressional Gold Medal in 1936. | Eric Arthur Blair, who was better known by his pen name George Orwell, was a British author who made a profound impact on literature. Just after Cohan died, Orwell wrote *Animal Farm,* a story of corruption, greed and ignorance. It is considered to be among the greatest English-language novels ever written. | In 1906, the world's first animated cartoon was released. In the same year, the first airplane flight in Europe took place in Paris, and the SOS international distress signal was adopted. |

## 2.5 YOU'RE A GRAND OLD FLAG ✏ *Circle the ♪♩♪ syncopations!*

George M. Cohan

## 2.5 YOU'RE A GRAND OLD FLAG – Timpani

George M. Cohan

*Timpani rolls are played using smooth, even single strokes. These should not be too fast.*

BB210PER

# BASS DRUM TECHNIQUE: ROLLS

**Bass drum rolls** are slow single strokes played 2–3 inches from the counterhoop of the drum. If the mallets are moved apart, keep them the same distance from the counterhoop for a smooth sound.

## 2.6 SUMMIT FANFARE

**Maestoso**

TRACK 1 • 39

## 2.7 THE FOREST OWL

Japanese Folk Song

**Misterioso**

TRACK 1 • 40

## 2.8 LITTLE BROWN JUG

Joseph E. Winner

**Moderato**

snares on

TRACK 1 • 41

BB210PER

**RHYTHM**
**13**
**2/4**

## CUT TIME (ALLA BREVE)

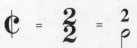

¢ = **2/2** = **2** 2 **beats** in each measure.
Half note gets one beat.

### 2.9 BEAT STREET – Duet

TRACK 1 42

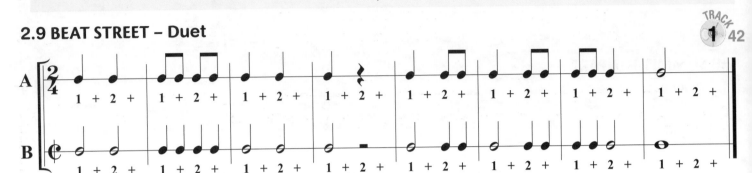

### 2.10 CUT IT OUT! *Notice how eighth notes are counted in cut time.*

TRACK 1 43

2 e + a

**HISTORY**

### MUSIC

**Modest Mussorgsky** (1839–1881) was a Russian composer whose music has a strong nationalistic flavor. The *Great Gate of Kiev* is the final movement of the larger work *Pictures at an Exhibition,* completed in 1874. It depicts a monumental gate designed for Tsar Alexander II.

### LITERATURE

In 1874, French author Victor Hugo, who is famous for the novels *Les Misérables* and *The Hunchback of Notre Dame,* wrote *Ninety-Three,* a novel set in 1793 during the French Revolution. Around the same time, William Wells Brown wrote *The Rising Sun.* Brown is considered the first African-American to have published a novel.

### WORLD

The first zoo in the U.S. opened in 1874 in Philadelphia, PA. Around the same time, P.T. Barnum's Circus (later to become the Barnum and Bailey Circus), the largest in the U.S., made its debut and began traveling the country by railroad.

### TAM-TAM

A **tam-tam** is a metal disc-shaped instrument that can be from 12 to 60 inches in diameter. **Tam-tams** are of indefinite pitch and are considered to have Mediterranean origins. **Gongs** are similar instruments that are of Asian origins and may be pitched. Both tam-tams and gongs are played by striking them just off center with a large, heavy mallet. The sound is stopped by pressing the mallet and the non-playing hand against both sides of the instrument. **Tam.** is the abbreviation used for tam-tam.

### 2.11 THE GREAT GATE OF KIEV

Modest Mussorgsky  TRACK 1 44

Pesante

*ff* 1 + a 2 +

Tam.

*ff* Cr. Cym.

11b

## 2.11 THE GREAT GATE OF KIEV – Timpani

Modest Mussorgsky

## 2.12 MANHATTAN BEACH

John Philip Sousa

BB210PER

12a

# STYLE AND FORM: TRIO

A **trio** has three different parts performed simultaneously by three individuals or groups.

## 2.13 MOOD CHANGE – Trio

## 2.14 CONCERT G NATURAL MINOR SCALE, ARPEGGIO AND CHORD

## 2.15 CONCERT G HARMONIC MINOR SCALE, ARPEGGIO AND CHORD

BB210PER

# TRIPLE PARADIDDLE

A **triple paradiddle** is a rudiment made of six single strokes followed by a double stroke.

Notice there is an accent on the first note.

13a

## 2.17 THE DRONING BAGPIPES

TRACK 1 50

## 2.18 CONCERTO THEME

Ludwig van Beethoven

TRACK 1 51

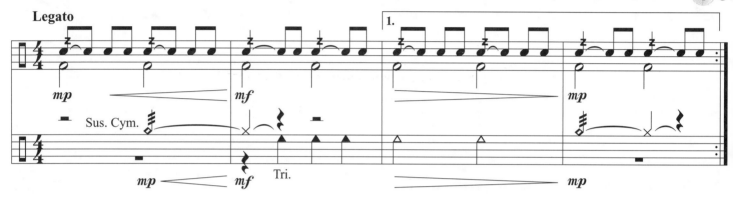

## 2.19 CHEKI, MORENA

Puerto Rican Dance

TRACK 1 52

BB210PER

## CUT TIME SYNCOPATION

Remember that weak beats are stressed in syncopation. Look at these examples.
Keeping a steady beat, clap and count the rhythm for each. They sound the same!

## 2.20 CHEKI, MORENA OTRA VEZ!

Puerto Rican Dance   TRACK 1 53

14a

## HISTORY

| MUSIC | | LITERATURE | WORLD |
|---|---|---|---|

**Camille Saint-Saëns** (1835–1921) was a French composer whose works included symphonic poems, symphonies and operas. *Bacchanale* is from the opera *Samson and Delilah,* completed in 1876. No opera house in France made any effort to stage it until Franz Listz helped arrange the first production a year later.

Anna Sewell's novel *Black Beauty* was published in 1877. It was Sewell's first and only novel. Since its publication, millions of readers have enjoyed this book, a horse's memoir. It has become one of the best-selling books in the world.

In 1877, Thomas Edison invented the Edisonphone, a tin cylinder phonograph that made the first recording. Also in 1877, the oldest tennis tournament in the world, Wimbledon, held its first men's tennis match.

## 2.21 BACCHANALE FROM SAMSON AND DELILAH

Camille Saint-Saëns

TRACK 1 54

## 2.21 BACCHANALE FROM SAMSON AND DELILAH – Timpani

Camille Saint-Saëns

TRACK 1 54

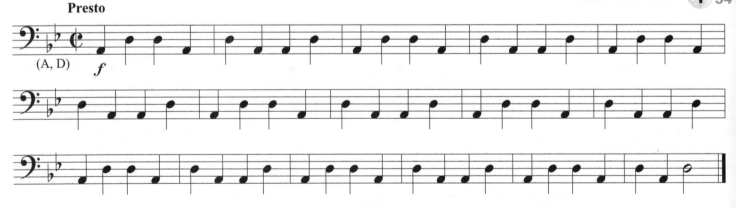

## TOM-TOM

A **tom-tom** is a drum that does not have snares and ranges in size from 6 to 18 inches. Tom-toms can have either a single head or double heads. They can be played with sticks, hard felt mallets, hard timpani mallets, or hard cord mallets. Though it can vary, they are often set up going left to right — low to high. **T.T.** is the abbreviation for tom-tom.

## 2.22 CHROMAT-ATTACK (FIGHT SONG) – Duet

TRACK 1 55

## IMPROVISATION

**Improvisation** occurs when performers compose and play music
on the spot, without rehearsal and without reading notation.

## 2.23 KLEZMER! – Improvisation

*Use the guide notes to improvise on a keyboard percussion instrument while your
partner plays the music below, or play along with the CD. You may also consider
using another percussion instrument and focus more on rhythmic improvisation.
(Note: The CD recording repeats 4 times.)*

TRACK 1 56

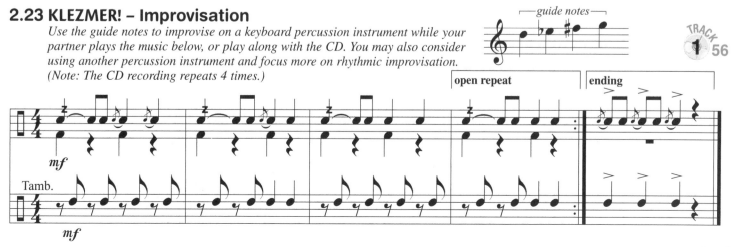

# OPUS 2 ENCORE!

## INTERPRETATION STATION

Listen to CD 1 Track 57. You will hear pairs of chords or scales. Listen to each pair, comparing the second example to the first. Decide if the second example in each pair is Major or minor. Circle your answers.

1. Major  minor        2. Major  minor        3. Major  minor        4. Major  minor

## SIMON "SEZ"

Listen to CD 1 Track 58. You will hear a well-known musical work. Listen first, sing it, then find the pitches on your keyboard percussion instrument. You can then play along with the accompaniment track that follows. Can you match the notes and style of the recording?

## COMPOSER'S CORNER

Using your knowledge of Major and minor, transform *London Bridge* into *Lonely Bridge* by rewriting it in a minor key. Think about which notes will need accidentals. The first two measures have already been completed for you!

### LONDON BRIDGE

Traditional

### LONELY BRIDGE

## PENCIL POWER – CREATING MAJOR AND MINOR CHORDS

Decide if the chord is Major or minor. Circle your answer. Be careful! Example 5 is tricky!

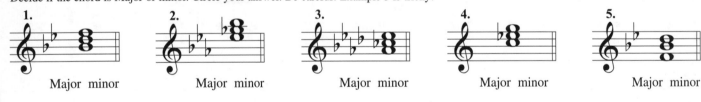

1. Major  minor        2. Major  minor        3. Major  minor        4. Major  minor        5. Major  minor

Correctly add notes to create the chord. Be careful! Example 10 is tricky!

6. E♭ Major        7. C Major        8. B♭ minor        9. A♭ Major        10. E♭ minor

## SIGHT READING

Sight reading is a way to demonstrate what you know about reading and performing music. Remember the **Three Ps** to help you sight read:

   **Preview:** Title, composer, key signature, time signature, tempo, style, articulation and expression markings
   **Process:** Imagine the flow of the music, silently sticking through transitions and complex passages
   **Perform:** Set your posture and grip, then play the passage as musically as possible

### 2.24 ELEMENTS – Sight Reading

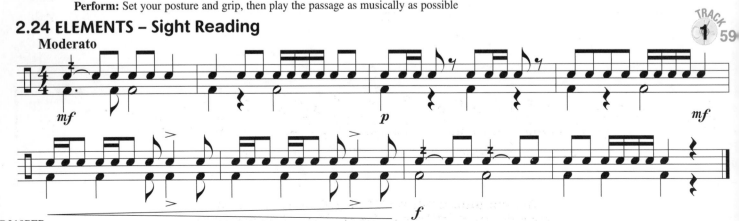

## 2.24a THE BROKEN BEETHOVEN MUSIC BOX – Percussion Ensemble
(Bells)

arr. Brian Balmages

BB210PER

15c

## 2.24a THE BROKEN BEETHOVEN MUSIC BOX – Percussion Ensemble
(Snare Drum, Bass Drum)

arr. Brian Balmages

BB210PER

15d

# RATCHET

The **ratchet** is an instrument that produces a strong "clicking sound." It is held in one hand and the handle is cranked with the other hand. Crank the handle for the duration of the note.

## 2.24a THE BROKEN BEETHOVEN MUSIC BOX – Percussion Ensemble
(Triangle, Tambourine, Suspended Cymbal, Crash Cymbals, Ratchet)*

arr. Brian Balmages

TRACK 1 64

* This part should be covered by 3 players. Player 1: Triangle; Player 2: Tambourine, Player 3: Suspended Cymbal, Crash Cymbals, Ratchet

BB210PER

# CURTAIN UP!

**2.25 MARCHE MILITAIRE** (Snare Drum, Bass Drum)

Franz Schubert
arr. Robert Sheldon

**2.25 MARCHE MILITAIRE** (Crash Cymbals)

Franz Schubert
arr. Robert Sheldon

## 2.26 SUNSET ON THE CHESAPEAKE (Triangle, Suspended Cymbal, Crash Cymbals)

Brian Balmages

Copyright © 2010 The FJH Music Company Inc. (ASCAP).
International Copyright Secured. Made in U.S.A. All Rights Reserved.

## 2.26a ETUDE FOR TWO TOM-TOMS

David Collier

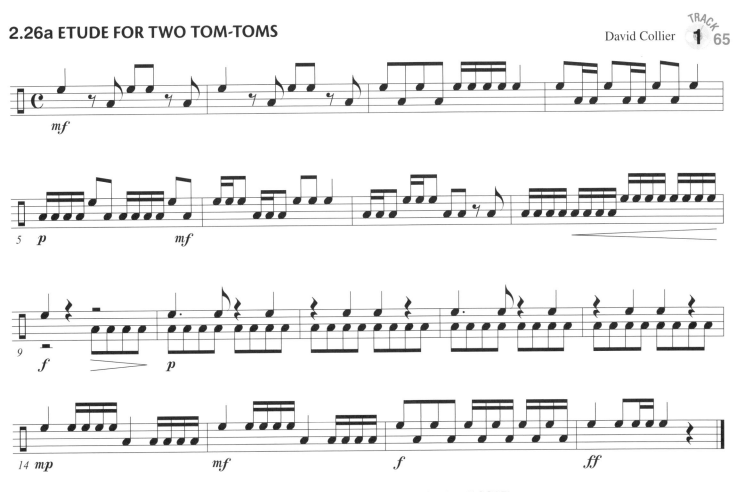

Copyright © 2011 The FJH Music Company Inc. (ASCAP).
International Copyright Secured. Made in U.S.A. All Rights Reserved.

BB210PER

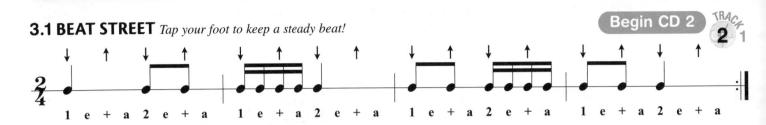

# ✳ OPUS 3

**3.1 BEAT STREET** *Tap your foot to keep a steady beat!*

Begin CD 2 — TRACK 2 / 1

1 e + a 2 e + a  1 e + a 2 e + a  1 e + a 2 e + a  1 e + a 2 e + a  1 e + a 2 e + a

**RUDIMENT**

## DOUBLE STROKE ROLLS

A **double stroke** is created by allowing the stick to bounce one time after each primary stroke. For each wrist motion, there are two clearly defined sounds. One double stroke by itself is called a **diddle.** Often, double strokes or diddles are added to sixteenth notes to produce **double stroke or rudimental rolls.** This is notated by placing a slash through a sixteenth note, two slashes through an eighth note, or 3 slashes through a quarter note or larger note value

### NINE STROKE ROLL

A **nine stroke roll** is created by playing four sixteenth notes with diddles plus a stroke at the end. This is often a **quarter note rudimental roll.**

### ✳ FOR PERCUSSION ONLY

**3.1a STREET BEAT — For Percussion Only**  TRACK 2 / 1

**3.2 SWEET SIXTEEN**  TRACK 2 / 2

**3.3 TSAR NIKOLAI**  Russian Folk Song  TRACK 2 / 3

## TRIANGLE TECHNIQUE: OPEN AND CLOSED

When holding the triangle clip correctly in the hand, it is possible to stop the sound by squeezing the ring and pinky fingers into the triangle. This produces a closed sound on the triangle when it is struck with a beater. When the ring and pinky finger are not touching the triangle, an open sound is produced when it is struck. An "o" means to play an open sound and a "+" means to play a closed sound.

open

closed

## 3.4 CARIBBEAN HOLIDAY

## 3.5 THE THUNDERER

John Philip Sousa

18a

## 3.6 BEAT STREET

## FIVE STROKE ROLL

A **five stroke roll** is created by playing two 16th notes with diddles plus a stroke at the end. This can happen on the first two 16th notes or the last two 16th notes. This is often an **eighth note rudimental roll.**

**FOR PERCUSSION ONLY**

## 3.6a STREET BEAT — For Percussion Only

## 3.7 16TH STREET

## 3.8 THE KING'S TRUMPETERS – Duet

Maestoso

BB210PER

## CONDUCTING REVIEW: ¾ TIME

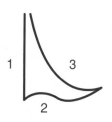

### 3.9 THE MATADOR

TRACK 2 9

### 3.9a ROLLING DOWN THE HIGHWAY — Snare Drum Solo

David Collier

TRACK 2 72

19a

## HISTORY

### MUSIC

*Trepak,* based on a Ukrainian folk dance, is part of the famous ballet *The Nutcracker,* written by **Pyotr I. Tchaikovsky** (1840–1893). Based on Hoffman's *The Nutcracker and the Mouse King,* it remains a favorite among listeners, especially during the holidays.

### LITERATURE

Scottish author Robert Louis Stevenson introduced the world to the fictitious pirate, Long John Silver, in his novel, *Treasure Island.* This adventure tells the tale of pirates and buried gold. Also, J.R.R. Tolkien, author of *The Hobbit* and *Lord of the Rings,* was born the same year *The Nutcracker* was premiered.

### WORLD

In 1892, Ellis Island became the official welcome center for immigrants to the U.S., Fig Newtons® were first produced and to make sure you had a sparkling smile after you ate them, the toothpaste tube was invented!

## TAMBOURINE TECHNIQUE: FIST-KNEE

When playing loud, fast passages that include sixteenth notes, we have to use a **fist-knee technique** on tambourine. Rest your foot on a chair or small box so that your knee is up. Hold the tambourine in your weaker hand with the head facing the floor over your knee. Use the fist of your stronger hand to play inside the tambourine (notated as F). Play the sixteenth notes between your fist and the top of your knee (notated as K).

### ✳ FOR PERCUSSION ONLY

## 3.10 TREPAK *Notice how flam taps occur on upbeats.*

Pytor I. Tchaikovsky — TRACK 2/10

## 3.10 TREPAK – Timpani *Remember to use single strokes on a timpani roll.*

Pytor I. Tchaikovsky — TRACK 2/10

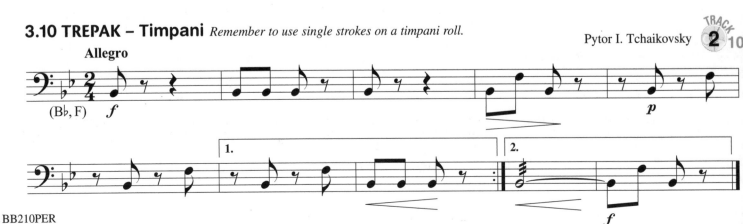

BB210PER

## 3.11 OLD JOE CLARK *Focus on using proper tambourine technique.*

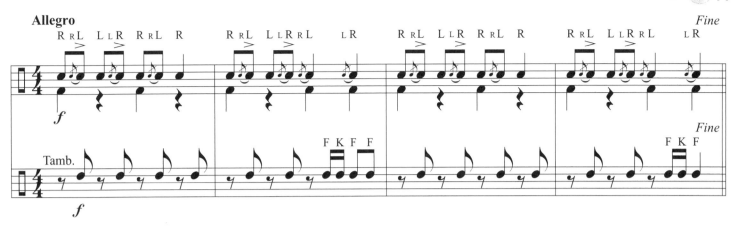

### MUSIC

*Green Bushes* is an English folk song that has been used by several composers. **Percy Grainger** (1882–1961) was a composer born in Australia who wrote some of the most notable works in the wind band literature. He used *Green Bushes* in several of his works including *Lincolnshire Posy* and *Green Bushes (Passacaglia on an English Folksong).*

### LITERATURE

The children's novel *A Little Princess* was written by Frances Hodgson Burnett. American author Jack London wrote his most famous novel, *The Call of the Wild,* a story about a domesticated dog that eventually turns back into a wild animal. London soon followed with a companion novel, *White Fang.*

### WORLD

Around the turn of the century, the Canadian provinces of Saskatchewan and Alberta were established. Front-wheel drive for automobiles was patented by a German engineer, and Las Vegas officially became a city in the U.S.

## 3.12 GREEN BUSHES

English Folk Song

## 3.13 BEAT STREET

## 3.13a STREET BEAT — For Percussion Only

## 3.14 ANOTHER WAY

## 3.15 STODOLA PUMPA

Czech Folk Song

**RUDIMENT**

### THIRTEEN STROKE ROLL

A **thirteen stroke roll** is created by playing six sixteenth notes with diddles plus a stroke at the end.
This is often a **dotted quarter note rudimental roll.**

## FOR PERCUSSION ONLY

BB210PER

### 3.16 LA MORISQUE

Tielman Susato

### 3.17 SKYWARD

### 3.18 THE MOREEN

Irish Air

ON THE PODIUM

CONDUCTING REVIEW: $\frac{2}{4}$ TIME

### 3.19 JIM ALONG JOSEY

American Folk Song

ON THE PODIUM

## 3.20 SQUARE DANCE – Duet

Moderato

### KEY CHANGE

A **key change** occurs when music moves from one key to another in a single musical work. You will know a key change has occurred when you see a double bar line followed by a new key signature. The new key signature shows the new sharps or flats and may also contain natural signs that cancel the sharps or flats from the previous key signature.

## 3.21 CHANGE UP (CONCERT F TO B♭ MAJOR)

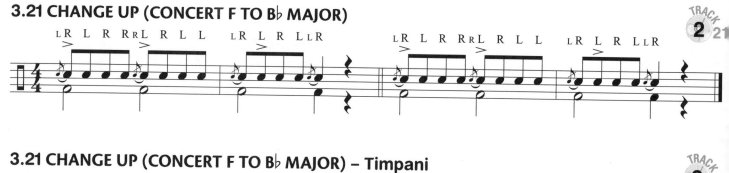

## 3.21 CHANGE UP (CONCERT F TO B♭ MAJOR) – Timpani

key change

(B♭, F)

# 3.22 DECK THE HALLS

Welsh Carol

# 3.22 DECK THE HALLS – Timpani

Welsh Carol

22a

RUDIMENT

## DRAG

The **drag**, or **ruff**, uses a double stroke, or diddle, on the grace notes. Notice the similarity with a flam. Keep the stick height of both grace notes low. Practice by first playing a flam and then diddling the grace note to produce a drag.

FOR PERCUSSION ONLY

## 3.23 CHILDREN'S PRAYER FROM HANSEL AND GRETEL

Engelbert Humperdinck

## 3.24 PATAPAN

Bernard de la Monnoye

## 3.24 PATAPAN – Timpani

Bernard de la Monnoye

BB210PER

# OPUS 3 ENCORE!

## INTERPRETATION STATION

**TRACK 2 · 28**

Listen to CD 2 Track 28. You will hear a tempo given by a click track. This is the speed of the quarter note. After each click track you will hear a rhythm. Select which notated rhythm is being played and write the corresponding answer letter on the line. Each example is performed twice.

1. _____    3. _____

2. _____    4. _____

## SIMON "SEZ"

**TRACK 2 · 29**

Listen to CD 2 Track 29. You will hear a well-known musical work. Listen first, sing it, then find the pitches on your keyboard percussion instrument. You can then play along with the accompaniment track that follows. Can you match the notes and style of the recording?

## COMPOSER'S CORNER

Many composers use key changes as a compositional technique. Rewrite this melody in the key of Concert E♭ Major. Then play the entire piece!

### SWEETLY SINGS THE DONKEY

Traditional

## PENCIL POWER

Rewrite the following musical examples using 5, 9, and 13 stroke rolls.

Rewrite this example showing the sixteenth note subdivision.

## SIGHT READING

Remember the Three Ps to help you sight read: **Preview, Process, Perform.**

### 3.28 LINE OF SIGHT – Sight Reading

**TRACK 2 · 30**

Moderato

*mf*

BB210PER

### 3.28a PRINCE WILLIAM'S MARCH – Timpani Solo

David Collier

TRACK **2** 73

# CURTAIN UP!

### 3.29 BARN DANCE (Snare Drum, Bass Drum)

Brian Balmages

### 3.29 BARN DANCE (Wood Block, Crash Cymbals)

Brian Balmages

## 3.30 CLOUDS (Suspended Cymbal, Triangle)

Robert Sheldon

TRACK **2** 32

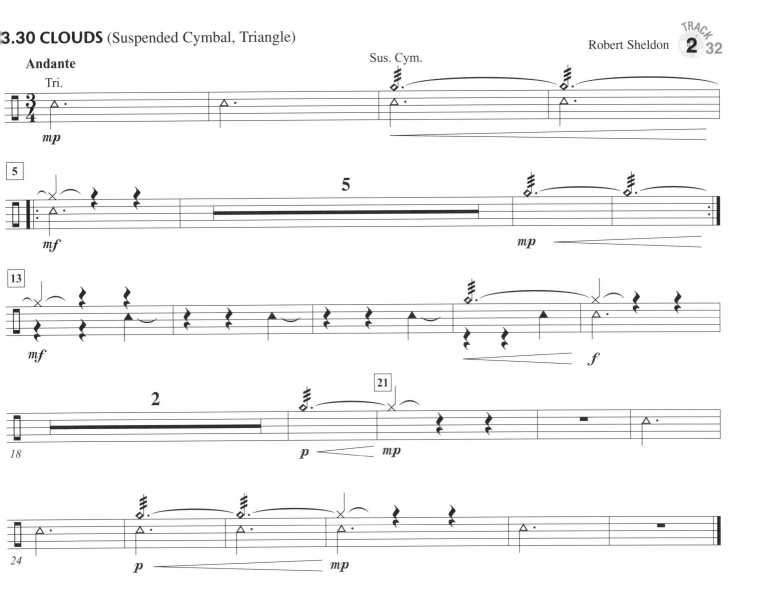

BB210PER

# ✳ OPUS 4

**RHYTHM**
**1 3**
**2 ⁴**

## MORE TIME SIGNATURES

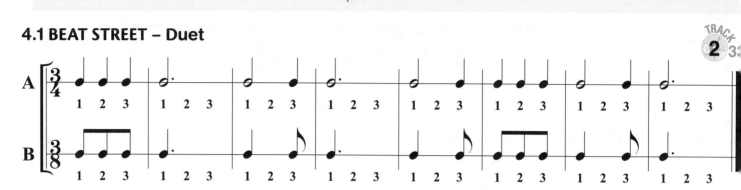

$\frac{3}{8}$ = **3** **3 beats** in each measure

Eighth note gets one beat

## 4.1 BEAT STREET – Duet

TRACK 2 33

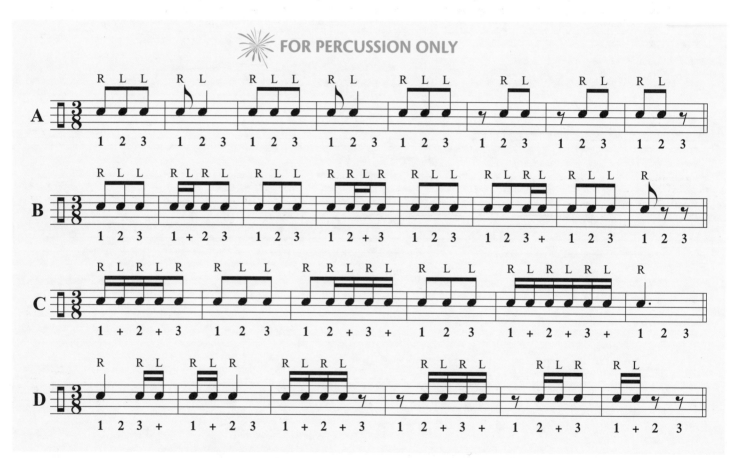

### ✳ FOR PERCUSSION ONLY

## 4.1a STREET BEAT — For Percussion Only

TRACK 2 33

## 4.2 TRIPLE THREAT

TRACK 2 34

## 4.3 POP! GOES THE WEASEL

English Traditional · TRACK 2 35

## 4.4 BRING A TORCH, JEANNETTE, ISABELLA

French Carol · TRACK 2 36

26a

## 4.5 PARADE OF THE WOODEN SOLDIERS – Duet

Leon Jessel

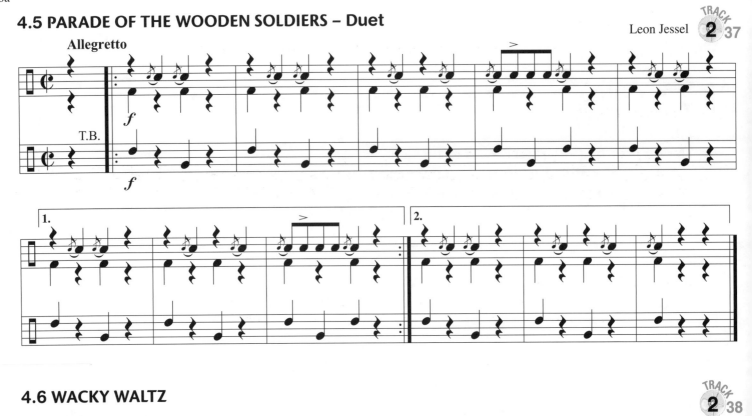

## 4.6 WACKY WALTZ

### DOUBLE STROKE ROLLS IN 3/8 TIME

Double stroke rolls are played the same regardless of time signature.
A diddle is added to the notes with slashes through the stems.

※ FOR PERCUSSION ONLY

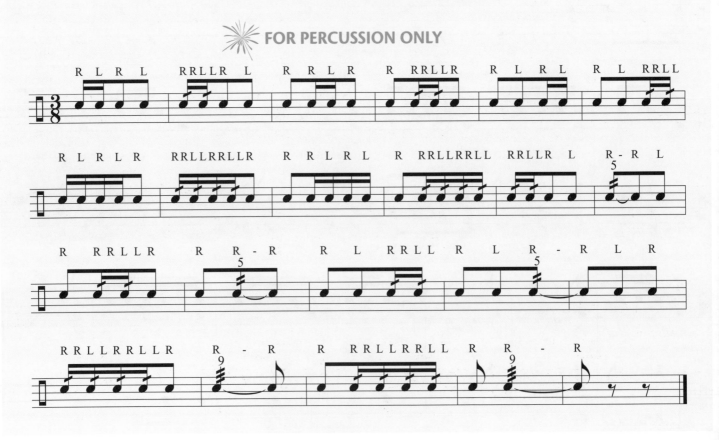

BB210PER

## RALLENTANDO

**Rallentando** – abbreviated "*rall.*" – means to gradually slow down, similar to ritardando (*rit.*).

### 4.7 DARK OVERTURE

## SINGLE DRAG TAP

The **single drag tap** is a combination of a drag followed by a single stroke.
It is similar to a flam tap but notice that the sticking is different. Be sure to diddle the grace notes.

### 4.8 TAFTA HINDI

Arabic Folk Song

### 4.9 À LA BAROQUE

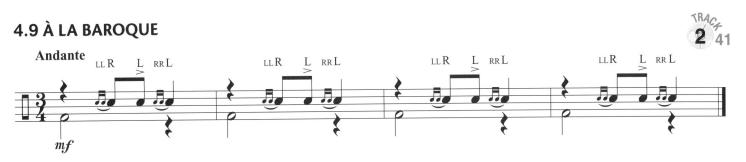

## 4.10 THE RAKES OF MALLOW

Irish Folk Song

**Allegretto**

ON THE PODIUM

## DRUM SET

The **drum set** is an instrument that grew out of the early ragtime music of New Orleans and is played by a single player. It has a bass drum played with a foot pedal, a snare drum, a floor tom, various mounted toms, a hi-hat, a ride cymbal and a crash cymbal. There are many variations to this setup. Drum set is heard in all types of commercial music such as rock, jazz, Latin, country, hip-hop and more.

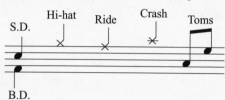

*Photograph courtesy of Yamaha Corporation of America*

THEORY

## D.C. AL CODA

Remember that D.C. is an abbreviation for *da capo*, an Italian term that refers to the beginning. A **coda** contains music that occurs at the end of a piece. **D.C. al Coda** means to return to the beginning and play until you come to the **coda sign**, ⊕. When you see the coda sign, skip to ⊕ **Coda** and play to the end.

## 4.11 GIVE MY REGARDS TO BROADWAY *Be sure to observe all the signs!*

George M. Cohan

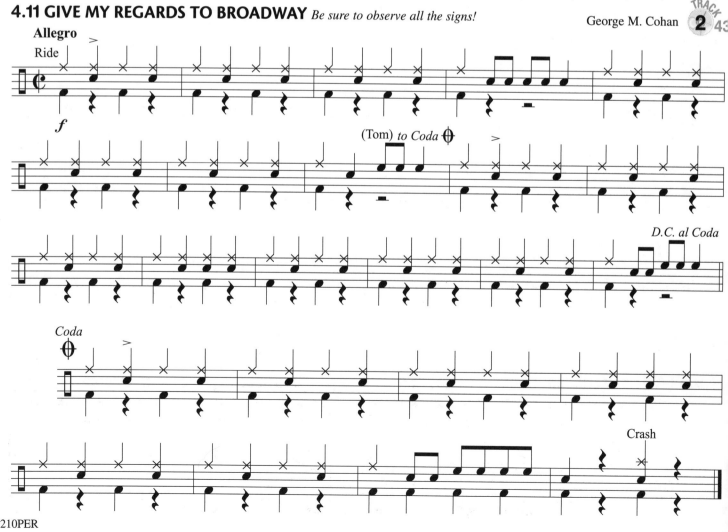

## 4.12 IN A FUNK

*Funk has roots in rhythm and blues. It was developed in the 1960s and 1970s and features strong bass lines.*

**TRACK 2 44**

Funk
closed Hi-hat
Drum Set
to Coda ⊕
*f*
> Ride
D.C. al Coda
Coda ⊕

## CONGAS

**Congas** are barrel shaped drums with a single head that are believed to have originated in the Niger-Congo region of West Africa. They were adapted into the existing native rumba music of Cuba to become a principal instrument in Afro-Cuban music. The three sizes are the *quinto, conga,* and *tumbadora* (or *tumba*) and they are played with the hands. Congas can be played standing if a stand is available, or seated by placing them on the floor. Strike the drum with fingers flat and together. The hand should strike the drum head with the knuckles lined up with the rim of the drum. For right-handed players, the small drum is on the left and the large drum is on the right.

## 4.12 IN A FUNK – Congas

**TRACK 2 44**

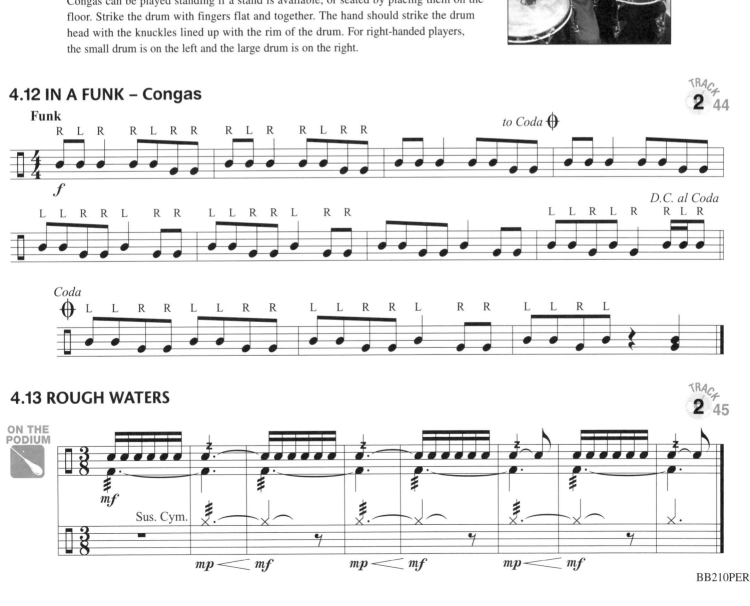

Funk
R L R   R L R R   R L R   R L R R
to Coda ⊕
*f*
L L R R L   R R   L L R R L   R R
D.C. al Coda
L L R L   R   R L R
Coda ⊕ L L R R L   L R R   L L R R L   R R   L L R L

## 4.13 ROUGH WATERS

**TRACK 2 45**

ON THE PODIUM

*mf*
Sus. Cym.

*mp* < *mf*     *mp* < *mf*     *mp* < *mf*

BB210PER

## MORE TIME SIGNATURES

$\frac{6}{8}$ = **6** **6 beats** in each measure
Eighth note gets one beat

In a faster tempo, emphasis is often placed on the 1st and 4th beats of each measure.
This gives the music a strong 2-beat pulse.

### 4.14 BEAT STREET

TRACK **2** 46

### 4.15 ROYAL FANFARE

**Maestoso**

TRACK **2** 47

### 4.16 LOOBY LOO *Conduct using a 2-beat pattern.*

Traditional    TRACK **2** 48

**ON THE PODIUM**

**Moderato**

### 4.17 UN CANADIEN ERRANT *Focus on flam accents in 6/8 time.*

French-Canadian Folk Song    TRACK **2** 49

**Andantino**

# 4.18 THE KERRY DANCE

Irish Folk Song

TRACK 2/50

## SIXTEENTH NOTES AND MULTIPLE BOUNCE ROLLS IN 6/8 TIME

Multiple bounce rolls are played the same way regardless of time signature.
Multiple bounce strokes are added to individual sixteenth notes to create rolls of various duration.

## ✳ FOR PERCUSSION ONLY

Practice this exercise in two-measure groupings.

Practice the following exercises by repeating each individual measure. Then play the entire exercise.

29

## 4.19 WALLABY STEW

Australian Folk Song

## 4.20 GRADUAL ASCENT

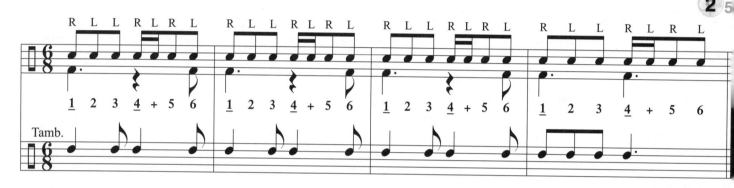

### HISTORY

**MUSIC**

**Bedřich Smetana** (1824–1884) was a musical hero to the Czech people. He wrote music with a very strong nationalistic flavor. *The Moldau*, premiered in 1875, is a movement of his larger work *Má vlast (My Motherland)*. It represents the beauty and strength of the great Bohemian Moldau river.

**LITERATURE**

American poet and master of the macabre Edgar Allan Poe, who died in 1849, was exhumed and reburied in 1875 in order to dedicate a grave marker to him. Almost fittingly, controversy still exists on whether or not the right body was reburied.

**WORLD**

In 1875, the English Channel was conquered by swimmer Matthew Webb. Folks with tummy troubles had new relief as Phillips'® Milk of Magnesia was introduced (it is still available in drug stores today!).

## 4.21 THEME FROM THE MOLDAU – Duet

Bedřich Smetana

BB210PER

## DOTTED EIGHTH NOTE/SIXTEENTH NOTE GROUP

Adding a dot after a note increases the length of the note by half of its value.
Here the dot is used with an eighth note to create a **dotted eighth note.**

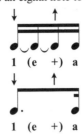

1 (e +) a

1 (e +) a

### 4.22 BEAT STREET – Duet

TRACK 2 54

### 4.22a STREET BEAT — For Percussion Only

TRACK 2 54

S.D. w/ snares off or T.T.

### 4.23 REGIMENT – Duet

TRACK 2 55

### 4.24 COUNTRY GARDENS

English Folk Song    TRACK 2 56

Allegretto

*mf*

## A TEMPO

The term **a tempo** means to return to the previous tempo.

### 4.25 LA DONNA È MOBILE

Giuseppe Verdi    TRACK 2 57

Moderato

*f*

*rall.*    *a tempo*

*p cresc.*    *f*

BB210PER

31a

**HISTORY**

**MUSIC**

**Richard Wagner** (1813–1883) was a German composer who wrote music noted for its rich harmonies and thick textures. Wagner's opera *Lohengrin*, first performed in 1850, contains the well-known *Wedding March* which is still a popular processional at many weddings.

**LITERATURE**

Poet Alfred Lord Tennyson became the United Kingdom's Poet Laureate in 1850. A high honor, the Poet Laureate is an official appointment bestowed by the government on a poet of great stature, who is called upon to write poems that commemorate important national events. In the U.S., American abolitionist and author Harriet Beecher Stowe wrote *Uncle Tom's Cabin*, sparking a national debate on slavery.

**WORLD**

In 1850, Australia's oldest university, the University of Sydney, was founded. At the same time, Harriet Tubman was deemed the official conductor of the Underground Railroad.

## 4.26 BRIDAL CHORUS FROM LOHENGRIN

Richard Wagner

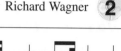

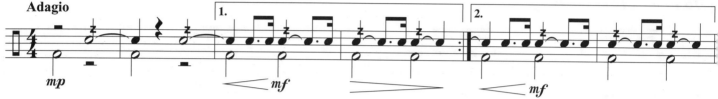

## 4.26 BRIDAL CHORUS FROM LOHENGRIN – Timpani

Richard Wagner

**HISTORY**

**MUSIC**

**Franz Schubert** (1797–1828) had only completed two movements of his *Symphony No. 8* ("Unfinished") before he left it for good. Other composers have offered versions of the complete symphony. No one really knows why Schubert did not finish the work. It is a musical mystery!

**LITERATURE**

Scottish author Sir Walter Scott wrote *Ivanhoe,* a novel in which Robin Hood made his first appearance. The story helped shape the modern concept of him as a cheerful, noble outlaw. At the same time, Catharine Sedgwick was writing novels and short stories in the United States. She was a champion of Republican motherhood, believing that mothers had a civic duty to raise children to be model citizens.

**WORLD**

In 1822, the United States officially recognized Mexico as an autonomous country. Dinosaur fossils and skeletons were discovered on the east coast of the U.S.

## 4.27 THEME FROM SYMPHONY NO. 8

Franz Schubert

BB210PER

# CASTANETS

**Castanets** are instruments of Moorish and Spanish origin and consist of a pair of concave disks. Traditionally they are played with a pair in each hand. In a concert setting, they are often mounted to a base to create **machine castanets,** which are played with the fingers of each hand. Each pair can also be attached to a handle to create **paddle castanets,** which are played against the raised thigh using both hands.

Machine Castanets

## 4.28 TARANTELLA

Italian Folk Song

## 4.29 CHANT – Improvisation

Use the guide notes provided to improvise on a keyboard percussion instrument while a partner plays the music below, or play along with the CD. You may also consider using another percussion instrument and focus more on rhythmic improvisation. *(Note: The CD recording repeats 4 times.)*

## 4.29 CHANT – Optional Drum Set

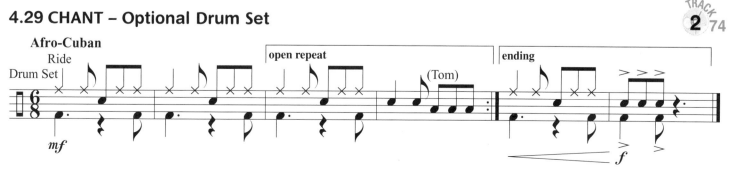

# OPUS 4 ENCORE!

## INTERPRETATION STATION

TRACK 2 62

Listen to CD 2 Track 62. For each example, determine the time signature. Circle your answer.

1. $\frac{2}{4}$ $\frac{3}{8}$     2. $\frac{6}{8}$ $\frac{4}{4}$     3. $\frac{3}{4}$ ¢     4. ¢ $\frac{3}{8}$

## SIMON "SEZ"

TRACK 2 63

Listen to CD 2 Track 63. You will hear a well-known musical work. Listen first, sing it, then find the pitches on your keyboard percussion instrument. You can then play along with the accompaniment track that follows. Can you match the notes and style of the recording?

## COMPOSER'S CORNER

Choose an instrument to play the B line of this duet. It can be bass drum, tom-tom, suspended cymbal with stick, or anything you prefer. Then, choose an instrument for the A line and complete the duet. Pair up with a friend and perform it for your class or family!

Title: _____     Composer: _____

## PENCIL POWER

Match each definition with its correct term or symbol by writing in the appropriate letter.

1. _____ Two beats in each measure; half note gets one beat

2. _____ Three or more pitches sounding simultaneously

3. _____ Three different parts performed simultaneously by three different individuals or groups

4. _____ Merry

5. _____ Playing music on the spot without rehearsal or notation

6. _____ Three beats in each measure; eighth note gets one beat

7. _____ Slightly slower than *Allegro*

8. _____ Coda

9. _____ Faster than *Allegro*

10. _____ Animated or lively

A. Animato

B. Presto

C. ⊕

D. Giocoso

E. $\frac{3}{8}$

F. Trio

G. Allegretto

H. ¢

I. Chord

J. Improvisation

## SIGHT READING

Remember the Three Ps to help you sight read: **Preview, Process, Perform.**

### 4.30 DANZA – Sight Reading

TRACK 2 64

# 4.30a AFRICANA – Accessory Percussion Ensemble
(Bongos, Cowbell)

Brian Balmages

TRACK **2** 75

32c

## 4.30a AFRICANA – Accessory Percussion Ensemble
(Maracas, Congas)

Brian Balmages

BB210PER

# 4.30a AFRICANA – Accessory Percussion Ensemble
(Claves, Tambourine)

Brian Balmages

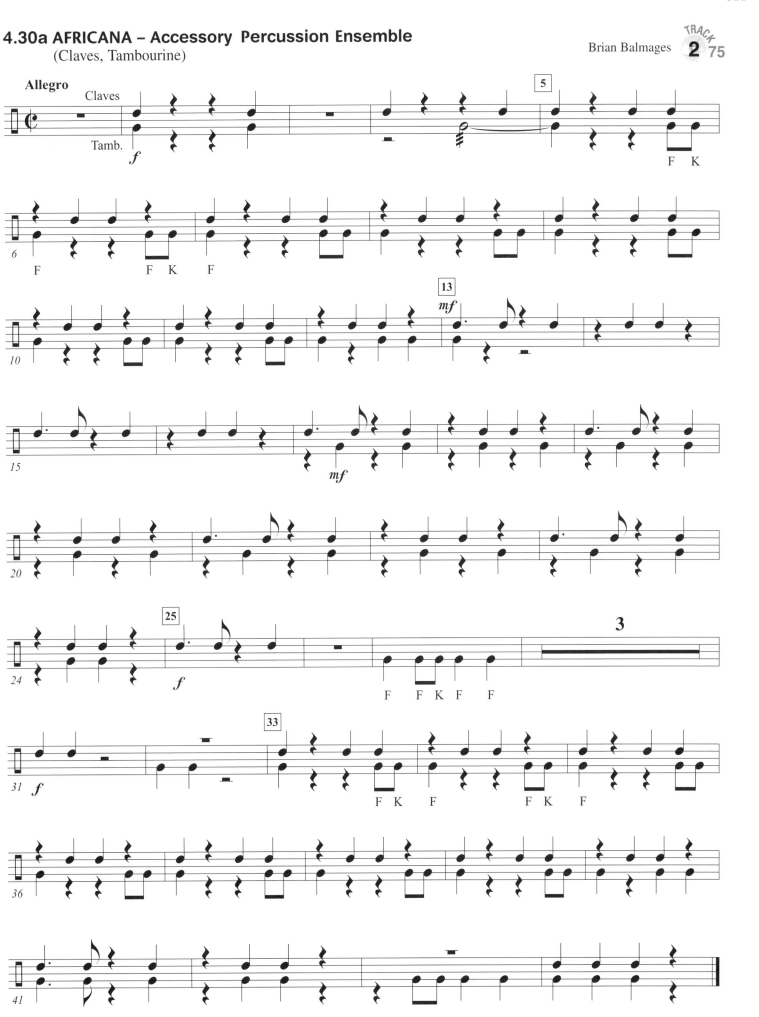

BB210PER

# CURTAIN UP!

**4.31 GARRYOWEN** (Snare Drum, Bass Drum)

*The jig, a popular dance originating in Ireland and Scotland, has a variety of repeated motions and is often set in 6/8 time.*

Irish Folk Song
arr. Robert Sheldon

TRACK 2 65

**4.31 GARRYOWEN** (Suspended Cymbal, Tom-toms)

Irish Folk Song
arr. Robert Sheldon

**Lively Jig**

**4.31 GARRYOWEN** (Timpani)

Irish Folk Song
arr. Robert Sheldon

**Lively Jig**

BB210PER

## 4.32 AMERICA, THE BEAUTIFUL (Snare Drum, Bass Drum)

*Molto is an Italian term that means "very much."*

Samuel A. Ward
arr. Brian Balmages

# BAR CHIMES

The **bar chimes** is an instrument made of graduated aluminum bars that are mounted horizontally. They produce a shimmering, glissando sound. They are played by gently dragging the fingers either left or right against the bars.

## 4.32 AMERICA, THE BEAUTIFUL (Bar Chimes, Suspended Cymbal, Crash Cymbals)

Samuel A. Ward
arr. Brian Balmages

TRACK 2 66

## 4.32 AMERICA, THE BEAUTIFUL (Timpani)

Samuel A. Ward
arr. Brian Balmages

TRACK 2 66

# OPUS 5

## 5.1 TOP OF THE MORNING

Moderato

TRACK 2 67

## 5.2 ENTER THE NOBLES

Maestoso

TRACK 2 68

Cr. Cym.

## 5.2 ENTER THE NOBLES — Timpani

Maestoso

TRACK 2 68

(A, E)

## DOTTED QUARTER NOTE/EIGHTH NOTE GROUP IN CUT TIME

Keeping a steady beat, clap and count the rhythm for each example. They sound the same!

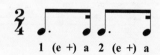

1 (e +) a   2 (e +) a

1 (e +) a   2 (e +) a

### 5.3 NOBLE PROCESSIONAL *Compare this piece to line 5.2. Do they sound the same?*

*Notice that double stroke rolls are notated with 2 slashes in cut time.*

### 5.3 NOBLE PROCESSIONAL — Timpani *Compare this piece to line 5.2. Do they sound the same?*

### 5.4 AIKEN DRUM

Scottish Folk Song

### 5.5 BLOW THE MAN DOWN

Sea Shanty

BB210PER

35a

## EIGHTH NOTE TRIPLETS

1 trip-let 2 trip-let

## 5.6 BEAT STREET

Begin CD 3  TRACK 3 1

## 5.7 TRIPLET FANFARE

TRACK 3 2

## SEVENTEEN STROKE ROLL

A **seventeen stroke roll** is created by playing eight sixteenth notes with diddles plus a stroke at the end.
This is often a **half note rudimental roll.**

## 5.8 FINALE FROM THE NEW WORLD SYMPHONY

Antonín Dvořák  TRACK 3 3

## 5.8 FINALE FROM THE NEW WORLD SYMPHONY — Timpani

Antonín Dvořák  TRACK 3 3

BB210PER

## 5.9 LIGHT CAVALRY OVERTURE

Franz von Suppé

## 5.10 STRIVE FOR FIVE This exercise combines single drag taps and rudimental rolls.

## 5.11 MOLLY MALONE

Irish Folk Song

36a

HISTORY

## MUSIC

**Antonio Vivaldi** (1678–1741) was a composer of the Baroque style. He was a highly skilled violinist and spent most of his life in Venice, Italy. *Autumn* is from a set of violin concertos entitled *The Four Seasons*. It was published in 1725. Vivaldi wrote each movement to be reminiscent of each season of the year.

## LITERATURE

Jonathan Swift was an Irish writer who was known as a master of satire. His novel *Gulliver's Travels* became incredibly popular as soon as it was published and continues to be one of his best-known works.

## WORLD

In 1723, Maryland required the establishment of public schools in all counties. A few years later across the Atlantic Ocean, France suffered from a famine and workers rioted when the price of bread was raised substantially. The coffeehouse craze was in full force in London, which had almost 2,000 of them!

## 5.12 AUTUMN FROM THE FOUR SEASONS

Antonio Vivaldi

TRACK 3

THEORY

## D.S. AL CODA

D.S. is an abbreviation for the Italian term *dal segno* or the sign, 𝄋. **D.S. al Coda** means to return to the sign (𝄋) and play until you come to the coda sign, 𝄌. When you see the coda sign, skip to the coda and play to the end.

## 5.13 DOWN BY THE STATION *Be sure to observe all the signs!*

American Folk Song

TRACK 38

## HISTORY

**MUSIC**

**Johann Strauss I** (1804–1849) was an Austrian composer whose legacy included many waltzes and the famous *Radetzky March,* which became quite popular among soldiers at the time. When Austrian officers first heard it, they clapped along with the chorus. This tradition is still carried on today.

**LITERATURE**

Alexandre Dumas, one of France's most renowned writers, wrote *The Queen's Necklace* in 1848. Dumas' most recognizable tales are *The Count of Monte Cristo* and *The Three Musketeers,* the latter telling of a young man named d'Artagnan who leaves home to become a guard of the musketeers.

**WORLD**

In 1848, the saxophone was patented, Spain opened its first railroad, and the first Women's Rights convention was held in New York.

## 5.14 RADETZKY MARCH

Johann Strauss I

## 5.14 RADETZKY MARCH — Timpani

Johann Strauss I

37a

## 5.15 MARCH CHROMATICA

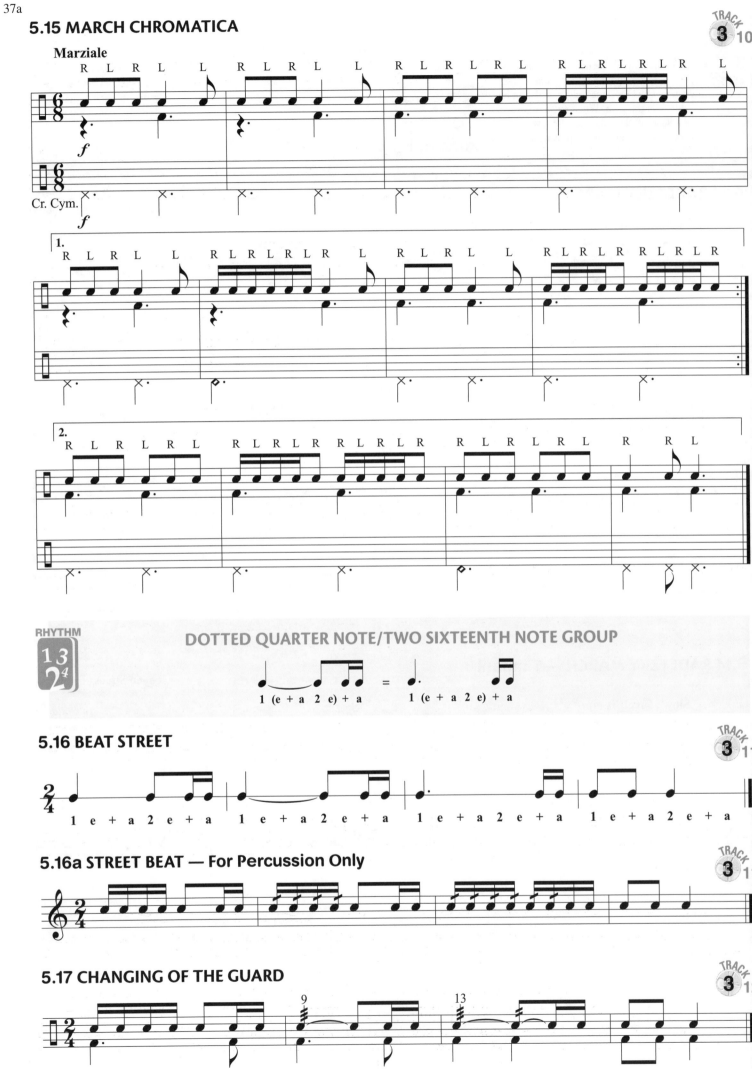

**DOTTED QUARTER NOTE/TWO SIXTEENTH NOTE GROUP**

## 5.16 BEAT STREET

## 5.16a STREET BEAT — For Percussion Only

## 5.17 CHANGING OF THE GUARD

## 5.18 OH! SUSANNA

Stephen C. Foster

**TRACK 3 13**

## 5.19 FINALE FROM SYMPHONY NO. 5

Pyotr I. Tchaikovsky

**TRACK 3 14**

## CRASH CYMBAL TECHNIQUE: SLIDE CRASH

The **slide crash** is a variation on the standard cymbal crash. It is produced by leaving the two cymbals lightly in contact with each other just after the crash. This produces a shimmering sizzle sound that extends the length of the crash and creates a unique timbre. The length of the contact can be from 1–2 seconds. Practice and experiment with this technique.

### 5.20 AN AUSTRIAN WENT YODELING

Austrian Folk Song

TRACK 3 15

### 5.21 MARYBOROUGH MINER

Australian Folk Song

TRACK 3 16

38b

## 5.22 SHABBAT SHALOM

Israeli Folk Song

## 5.23 BATTLE HYMN OF THE REPUBLIC

Traditional American Melody

## 5.24 BLUES ROCK – Improvisation

The guide notes provided form a blues scale. Play the notes moving up and down a few times. Then use the notes to improvise your own melody. You may also consider using another percussion instrument, including drum set, and focus more on rhythmic improvisation. Have a friend play the accompaniment part or play along with the accompaniment track on the CD. Have fun! (Note: The CD recording repeats 3 times.)

BB210PER

# OPUS 5 ENCORE!

## INTERPRETATION STATION

Listen to CD 3 Track 20. Each example uses one of the musical elements below. Write the corresponding letter in the space provided.

1. _____   2. _____   3. _____   4. _____

**A.** Diminuendo   **B.** Molto ritardando   **C.** Eighth note triplets   **D.** Sixteenth notes

## SIMON "SEZ"

Listen to CD 3 Track 21. You will hear a well-known musical work. Listen first, sing it, then find the pitches on your keyboard percussion instrument. You can then play along with the accompaniment track that follows. Can you match the notes and style of the recording?

## COMPOSER'S CORNER

Compose a piece using at least three different percussion instruments that can be played by one person. Assign each instrument to its own line or space before you begin. *Hint: Don't forget the D.S. al Coda!*

Title: _____    Composer: _____

*D.S. al Coda*    *Coda*

## PENCIL POWER

Study each example and decide its time signature. Write the time signature in the appropriate place on the staff.

**1.**

**2.**

**3.** *Two time signatures will work for this example. Use both.*

**4.** *Bonus: This example uses a time signature that you have never seen. Can you figure it out?*

## SIGHT READING

Remember the Three Ps to help you sight read: **Preview, Process, Perform.**

### 5.25 INTRADA – Sight Reading

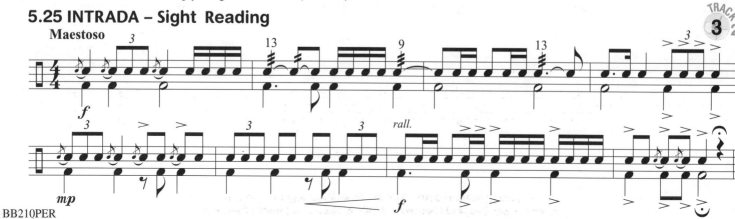

# CURTAIN UP! FULL BAND

## 5.26 TURKISH MARCH FROM THE RUINS OF ATHENS
(Snare Drum, Bass Drum)

Ludwig van Beethoven
arr. Brian Balmages

TRACK 3 23

## 5.26 TURKISH MARCH FROM THE RUINS OF ATHENS
(Triangle, Crash Cymbals)

Ludwig van Beethoven
arr. Brian Balmages

TRACK 3 23

## 5.27 CIRCUS DAZE (Snare Drum, Bass Drum)

Robert Sheldon

TRACK **3** 24

## 5.27 CIRCUS DAZE (Crash Cymbals, Triangle, Slide Whistle)

Robert Sheldon

## 5.27 CIRCUS DAZE (Timpani)

Robert Sheldon

BB210PER

# ✳ OPUS 6

**RHYTHM**
**13**
**2⁴**

## METER CHANGES

You have already played pieces with variations that use a meter change.
Sometimes the meter can change within the main melody. Remember these hints:

- Look ahead as you play.
- Check the bottom number of each time signature to determine what kind of note gets one beat.
- Watch your conductor!

### 6.1 PROMENADE FROM PICTURES AT AN EXHIBITION *Bonus: Conduct this piece!*

Modest Mussorgsky

**TRACK 3** 25

**ON THE PODIUM**

Moderato

*f*

### 6.2 FUM, FUM, FUM

Spanish Carol

**TRACK 3** 26

Moderato

*mf*

*f*

**RHYTHM**
**13**
**2⁴**

## SIXTEENTH NOTE TRIPLETS

**Sixteenth note triplets** are very similar to eighth note triplets. They are produced by playing three sixteenth notes for every eighth note. Use the syllables "dig-a-da" when counting each sixteenth note triplet.

dig- a - da  dig - a - da

### ✳ FOR PERCUSSION ONLY

A
1   +   dig-a-da   +   3   +   dig-a-da   +       1   +   2   dig-a-da  3   dig-a-da  4   +

B
1   +   2   +   3   dig-a-da  4   dig-a-da       1   +   dig-a-da-dig-a-da  3   +   dig-a-da  +

## 6.3 SHENANDOAH

American Folk Song

TRACK **3** 27

Espressivo

## 6.4 SLITHERY SNAKE

TRACK **3** 28

## 6.5 NIGHT ON BALD MOUNTAIN

Modest Mussorgsky

TRACK **3** 29

Pesante

42a

## 6.6 MARCH OF THE TOREADORS

Georges Bizet

## 6.7 O TANNENBAUM

German Folk Song

## 6.8 MOUNTAIN CLIMBING

## 6.9 THE BRITISH GRENADIERS *Remember that double stroke rolls only have two slashes in cut time.*

English Marching Song

BB210PER

## HISTORY

### MUSIC

English composer **Sir Edward Elgar** (1857–1934) was one of the first composers to take advantage of new technology by recording many of his works to phonograph discs in the early 1900s. His famous march *Pomp and Circumstance* was premiered in 1901 and is often heard at graduation ceremonies.

### LITERATURE

In 1901, American naturalist John Muir published *Our National Parks,* a collection of essays that helped conservation advocacy. *The Tale of Peter Rabbit* was privately published by Beatrix Potter. It was so successful that a publishing company accepted it a year later.

### WORLD

British engineer Hubert Booth invented and patented a horse-drawn, house-to-house vacuum cleaner. William S. Harley created a drawing of an engine designed to fit a bicycle. This would be the prototype of the first Harley motorcycle.

## 6.10 POMP AND CIRCUMSTANCE

Sir Edward Elgar  TRACK 3 34

**Stately**

## 6.10a A SOLDIER'S SALUTE – Snare Drum Solo

David Collier  TRACK 3 50

BB210PER

43a

## 6.11 MARCH FROM THE NUTCRACKER

Pytor I. Tchaikovsky

TRACK 3 35

## 6.12 WHEN JOHNNY COMES MARCHING HOME

American Folk Song

TRACK 3 36

**MUSIC**

*Blow Away the Morning Dew* (also known as *The Baffled Knight*) is an English folk song dating back to the early 1600s. British composer **Ralph Vaughan Williams** (1872–1958) used it as one of the main melodies in the third movement of *English Folk Song Suite,* which he wrote for military band in 1923.

**LITERATURE**

In 1911, English playwright and author Frances Hodgson Burnett published *The Secret Garden,* which has become a classic of children's literature. In 1923, Austrian author Felix Salten wrote the novel *Bambi, A Life in the Woods.* This went on to become a successful Disney animated feature.

**WORLD**

*Time* magazine was first published in 1923. It was a big year for candy lovers. Reese's® Peanut Butter Cups, Butterfinger®, and Milky Way® bars were all invented!

## 6.13 BLOW AWAY THE MORNING DEW

English Folk Song

TRACK 3 37

BB210PER

# 6.13a NUTS AND BOLTS — Multiple Percussion Solo
(3 Tom-toms, Wood Block, Suspended Cymbal)

David Collier

TRACK 3 · 51

*Note that 10, 12 and 14 inch tom-toms are recommended.*
*Also, a small (14–16") cymbal is suggested.*

**Moderato**

play w/ medium hard cord or yarn mallets

BB210PER

44

**HISTORY**

## MUSIC

**Nikolai Rimsky-Korsakov** (1844–1908) was a Russian composer who was also a master of orchestration. *Procession of the Nobles* is from the opera *Mlada,* which had a score that was divided between several composers. The entire project was never completed, yet this remains a popular work.

## LITERATURE

American author Stephen Crane wrote the war novel *The Red Badge of Courage* in 1895. The story illustrates the harshness of the American Civil War and has become one of the most influential works in American literature. Ironically, Crane was not born until after the war ended.

## WORLD

In 1895, Caroline Willard Baldwin became the first woman to earn a doctor of science degree at Cornell University. Around the same time, William Wrigley Jr. introduced Juicy Fruit® and Wrigley's Spearmint® chewing gum.

### 6.14 PROCESSION OF THE NOBLES

*Pomposo (grand and dignified)*

Nikolai Rimsky-Korsakov

TRACK 3

### 6.15 THE STAR-SPANGLED BANNER

*Stately*

U.S. National Anthem

TRACK 3 39

### 6.16 "FINISHED THE BOOK" BLUES – Improvisation

*As in Opus 5, the guide notes provided form a blues scale. The drum set part provided is an example of what a drummer would play in a swing tune. As the music indicates, practice swinging the eighth notes so they have more of a triplet feel. (Note: The CD recording repeats 2 times.)*

TRACK 3 40

BB210PER

# OPUS 6 ENCORE!

## INTERPRETATION STATION

Listen to CD 3 Track 41. For each example, decide which term best fits the music. Circle your answer.

| 1. Espressivo | 2. Pesante | 3. Marziale | 4. Giocoso |
|---|---|---|---|
| Maestoso | Andantino | Legato | Cantabile |

## SIMON "SEZ"

Listen to CD 3 Track 42. You will hear a well-known musical work. Listen first, sing it, and then find the pitches on your keyboard percussion instrument. You can then play along with the accompaniment track that follows. Can you match the notes and style of the recording?

## COMPOSER'S CORNER

Compose a piece using at least three different percussion instruments that can be played by one person. Assign each instrument to its own line or space before you begin. Make sure that you have the correct number of beats in each measure by paying attention to the meter changes. Don't forget to add dynamics and articulations. Title your piece and perform it for family and friends.

Title: _____  Composer: _____

## PENCIL POWER – MATCH THE COMPOSER

Match each composition with its composer by writing in the appropriate letter. Be careful! There are more composers than there are compositions!

1. _____ Trepak
2. _____ Bacchanale from Samson and Delilah
3. _____ La Donna è Mobile
4. _____ Pomp and Circumstance
5. _____ Hungarian Dance No. 5
6. _____ Procession of the Nobles
7. _____ The Great Gate of Kiev
8. _____ The Moldau
9. _____ Bridal Chorus from Lohengrin
10. _____ Give My Regards to Broadway

A. Elgar
B. Mussorgsky
C. Wagner
D. Smetana
E. Saint-Saëns
F. Offenbach
G. Cohan
H. Rimsky-Korsakov
I. Tchaikovsky
J. Brahms
K. Verdi
L. Strauss

## SIGHT READING

Remember the Three Ps to help you sight read: **Preview, Process, Perform.**

### 6.17 CHANGES – Sight Reading

BB210PER

# CURTAIN UP!

**6.18 ZIMBABWE!** (Snare Drum, Bass Drum)

Robert Sheldon

46c

## 6.18 ZIMBABWE! (Tambourine, Cowbell)

Robert Sheldon

TRACK 3/4

BB210PER

# 6.19 FIREBOLT FANFARE (Snare Drum, Bass Drum)

Brian Balmages

TRACK **3** 45

BB210PER

47b

## 6.19 FIREBOLT FANFARE (Triangle, Crash Cymbals, Suspended Cymbal)

Brian Balmages

TRACK 3 45

BB210PER

# 6.20a DREAMING OF SUMMER – Percussion Ensemble (Xylophone)

Brian Balmages

TRACK **3** 52

BB210PER

## 6.20a DREAMING OF SUMMER – Percussion Ensemble
(Marimba 1 or Opt. Vibraphone)

Brian Balmages

TRACK **3** 52

**Calypso**
medium yarn mallets

# 6.20a DREAMING OF SUMMER – Percussion Ensemble (Marimba 2)

Brian Balmages

TRACK 3 52

**Calypso**

Play one octave lower than written.
medium yarn mallets

BB210PER

# 6.20a DREAMING OF SUMMER – Percussion Ensemble (Congas)

Brian Balmages

## GUIRO

The **guiro** (GWEE-roe) is a scraped percussion instrument that is found in the music of Latin and South America. In its traditional form, it is made from a hollow dried gourd with ridges cut in the top. Today, many are made from plastic. It is played by scraping a small thin stick (or dowel) down (**D**) and up (**U**) across the ridges to create the rhythms. The length of the stroke is often determined by the length of the note in the music.

# 6.20a DREAMING OF SUMMER – Percussion Ensemble
(Claves, Maracas, Guiro)

Brian Balmages  **3** 52

BB210PER

# SCALES AND TECHNIQUE

Percussionists have six options on these pages, each which focuses on different skills and accessory percussion.
Your director will tell you which option you should play while the rest of the band plays their scales.

## OPTION 1

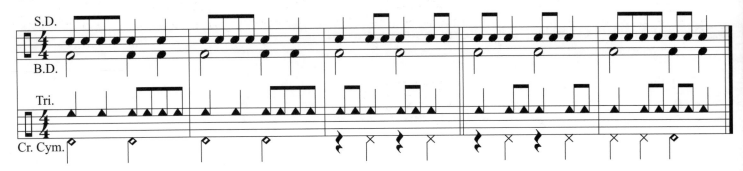

## OPTION 2

## OPTION 3

## OPTION 4

## OPTION 5

## OPTION 6

# RHYTHM REVIEW FOR PERCUSSION – OPUS 1-6

An additional rhythm review can be found in the keyboard percussion side of your book on page 52.

53

BB210PER

# P.A.S. 40 INTERNATIONAL SNARE DRUM RUDIMENTS

## I. ROLL RUDIMENTS

### A. SINGLE STROKE ROLL RUDIMENTS

#### 1. SINGLE STROKE ROLL

R L R L R L R L

#### 2. SINGLE STROKE FOUR

R L R L    R L R L
L R L R    L R L R

#### 3. SINGLE STROKE SEVEN

R L R L R L R
L R L R L R L

### B. MULTIPLE BOUNCE ROLL RUDIMENTS

#### 4. MULTIPLE BOUNCE ROLL

#### 5. TRIPLE STROKE ROLL

R R R L L L R R R L L L

### C. DOUBLE STROKE OPEN ROLL RUDIMENTS

#### 6. DOUBLE STROKE OPEN ROLL

R R L L R R L L

#### 7. FIVE STROKE ROLL

R   R   L   L

#### 8. SIX STROKE ROLL

R   L R   L
L   R L   R

#### 9. SEVEN STROKE ROLL

R   L R   L
L   R L   R

#### 10. NINE STROKE ROLL

R   R   L   L

#### 11. TEN STROKE ROLL
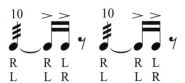
R   R L   R   R L
L   L R   L   L R

#### 12. ELEVEN STROKE ROLL

R   R L   R   R L
L   L R   L   L R

#### 13. THIRTEEN STROKE ROLL

R    R L    L

#### 14. FIFTEEN STROKE ROLL

R    L R    L
L    R L    R

#### 15. SEVENTEEN STROKE ROLL
R   R   L   L

Reprinted by permission of the Percussive Arts Society, Inc.
32 E. Washington, Suite 1400, Indianapolis, IN 46204-3516;
Email: percarts@pas.org; Web: www.pas.org.

## II. DIDDLE RUDIMENTS

### 16. SINGLE PARADIDDLE

R L R R L R L L

### 17. DOUBLE PARADIDDLE

R L R L R R L R L R L L

### 18. TRIPLE PARADIDDLE

R L R L R L R R L R L R L R L L

### 19. SINGLE PARADIDDLE-DIDDLE

R L R R L L R L R R L L
L R L L R R L R L L R R

## III. FLAM RUDIMENTS

### 20. FLAM

L R    R L

### 21. FLAM ACCENT

L R L R r L R L

### 22. FLAM TAP

L R R r L L L R R r L L

### 23. FLAMACUE

L R L R L L R
r L R L R r L

### 24. FLAM PARADIDDLE

L R L R R r L R L L

### 25. SINGLE FLAMMED MILL

L R R L R r L L R L

### 26. FLAM PARADIDDLE-DIDDLE

L R L R R L L L r L R L L R R

### 27. PATAFLAFLA

L R L R r L L R L R r L

### 28. SWISS ARMY TRIPLET

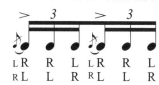

L R R L L R R L
r L L R r L L R

### 29. INVERTED FLAM TAP

L R L r L R L R L r L R

### 30. FLAM DRAG

L R L L R r L R R L

# IV. DRAG RUDIMENTS

### 31. DRAG

### 32. SINGLE DRAG TAP

### 33. DOUBLE DRAG TAP

### 34. LESSON 25

### 35. SINGLE DRAGADIDDLE

### 36. DRAG PARADIDDLE #1

### 37. DRAG PARADIDDLE #2

### 38. SINGLE RATAMACUE

### 39. DOUBLE RATAMACUE

### 40. TRIPLE RATAMACUE

# INDEX

BB210PER

# PERCUSSION INDEX

# CMS/ARROYO BAND PRACTICE CHART 2019-2020

First Name: Kyle    Last Name: Williams    Class: 4    Week #: 2

185

Log the number of minutes you practiced each week in the appropriate boxes. *You must write in pen.*

| Monday | Tuesday | Wednesday | Thursday | Friday | Saturday | Sunday |
|--------|---------|-----------|----------|--------|----------|--------|
| 20 | 15 | 15 | 15 | 26 | 15 | 15 |
| 15 | 15 | 15 | 20 | 15 | 15 | 15 |

110

225

Parent Signature: _____    Total minutes practiced: 225

Requirements:
- Students must practice at least 100 minutes per week for at least 3 days/week. 5 days for 20 minutes is ideal.
- Practice sessions that are less than 15 minutes long will not receive credit.
- Charts are due on Mondays every other week, and will not be accepted more than one week late.
- Late practice charts will have a grade reduction.

|--------|---------|-----------|----------|--------|----------|--------|
| | | | | | | |
| | | | | | | |

# MEASURES

*of*

# SUCCESS®

## A Comprehensive Musicianship Band Method

INCLUDES 2
PLAY-ALONG CDs

DEBORAH A. SHELDON

BRIAN BALMAGES

TIMOTHY LOEST

ROBERT SHELDON

PERCUSSION WRITTEN AND EDITED

BY DAVID COLLIER

THE
F·J·H
MUSIC
COMPANY
INC.
Frank J. Hackinson

# PRACTICE LOG

| Week | Date | Assignment | Mon | Tue | Wed | Thur | Fri | Sat | Sun | Total | Parent Initials |
|------|------|------------|-----|-----|-----|------|-----|-----|-----|-------|-----------------|
| 1 | | | | | | | | | | | |
| 2 | | | | | | | | | | | |
| 3 | | | | | | | | | | | |
| 4 | | | | | | | | | | | |
| 5 | | | | | | | | | | | |
| 6 | | | | | | | | | | | |
| 7 | | | | | | | | | | | |
| 8 | | | | | | | | | | | |
| 9 | | | | | | | | | | | |
| 10 | | | | | | | | | | | |
| 11 | | | | | | | | | | | |
| 12 | | | | | | | | | | | |
| 13 | | | | | | | | | | | |
| 14 | | | | | | | | | | | |
| 15 | | | | | | | | | | | |
| 16 | | | | | | | | | | | |
| 17 | | | | | | | | | | | |
| 18 | | | | | | | | | | | |
| 19 | | | | | | | | | | | |
| 20 | | | | | | | | | | | |
| 21 | | | | | | | | | | | |
| 22 | | | | | | | | | | | |
| 23 | | | | | | | | | | | |
| 24 | | | | | | | | | | | |
| 25 | | | | | | | | | | | |
| 26 | | | | | | | | | | | |
| 27 | | | | | | | | | | | |
| 28 | | | | | | | | | | | |
| 29 | | | | | | | | | | | |
| 30 | | | | | | | | | | | |
| 31 | | | | | | | | | | | |
| 32 | | | | | | | | | | | |
| 33 | | | | | | | | | | | |
| 34 | | | | | | | | | | | |
| 35 | | | | | | | | | | | |
| 36 | | | | | | | | | | | |

# MEASURES *of* SUCCESS®

## A Comprehensive Musicianship Band Method

DEBORAH A. SHELDON • BRIAN BALMAGES • TIMOTHY LOEST • ROBERT SHELDON

PERCUSSION WRITTEN AND EDITED BY DAVID COLLIER

Congratulations on completing the first book of *Measures of Success,* and welcome to Book 2! Throughout this book, you will explore music from many different countries around the world and learn about many composers that you did not encounter in Book 1. You will also explore some of the fascinating historical events and literature that help bring the days of these composers to life.

This book includes 2 accompaniment CDs that contain performance tracks with live musicians playing the music from your book, as well as accompaniment tracks so you can play along. Additional CDs that cover the remainder of the book can be purchased at your local music dealer or downloaded at www.fjhmusic.com/mos.

Enjoy this exciting time in your musical growth. As you practice, you will continue to find yourself sharing the gift of music with family, friends, and audiences.

Ready?

Let's make music!

## ABOUT THIS BOOK

Similar to Book 1, this book is divided into two main sections. The first section includes snare drum, bass drum, accessory percussion and timpani. These pages are often divided into A and B pages because there are multiple instruments you will learn. The second section contains all of the keyboard percussion exercises. Be sure to work from both sides of the book so that you become a *complete percussionist!* Finally, look at the last page of the book for a list of **recommended sticks and mallets.**

Production: Frank J. Hackinson
Production Coordinators: Ken Mattis and Brian Balmages
Cover Design and Interior Line Drawings: Danielle Taylor and Adrianne Hirosky
Interior Layout and Design: Andi Whitmer
Engraving: Tempo Music Press, Inc.
Printer: Tempo Music Press, Inc.

ISBN-13: 978-1-56939-902-6

THE
F·J·H
MUSIC
COMPANY
INC.
Frank J. Hackinson

# PRELUDE: THE WARM-UP

The **warm-up** prepares you for individual practice or rehearsal. Much as an athlete warms up before an event, musicians must do the same thing. Play these exercises with and without the CD each time you practice. Even as they become easier, focus on playing with a beautiful sound.

## 1. STEADY AS SHE GOES

## 2. SOUND BUILDER

## 3. HALF AND HALF

## 4. CHORALE – Trio or Full Band

## 5. CHORALE (BEFIEHL DU DEINE WEGE) – Full Band

J.S. Bach

BB210PER

# ✴ OPUS 1: RECAPITULATION

A **recapitulation** is a summary that restates the main points of a subject. In music, a recapitulation occurs after a development section and presents the main themes of a movement for a final time. Your musicianship developed substantially in Book 1, so the following recapitulation will reacquaint you with many of the concepts you have already learned.

## LET'S REVIEW

The following music will help you to remember these important elements:

### 1.1 GIVE ME FIVE!

### 1.2 SUR LE PONT D'AVIGNON
French Folk Song

### 1.3 THIS OLD MAN
English Folk Song

### 1.4 ORANGES AND LEMONS
English Folk Song

### 1.5 THEME FROM SONATA NO. 11
Wolfgang Amadeus Mozart

4

The following music will help you to remember these important elements:

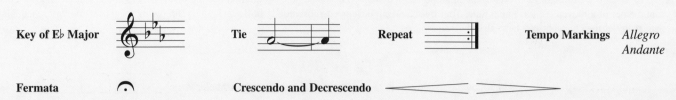

Key of E♭ Major    Tie    Repeat    Tempo Markings *Allegro* *Andante*

Fermata    Crescendo and Decrescendo

### 1.6 FADING FANFARE

TRACK 1 12

### 1.7 AURA LEE

American Folk Song

TRACK 1 13

### 1.8 LOS POLLITOS

Mexican Folk Song

TRACK 1 14

**Allegro**

HISTORY

## MUSIC

Polish composer **Frédéric Chopin** (1810–1845), much like Mozart, was a musical prodigy who began composing at a very early age. He was an accomplished pianist and all of his works involve the piano. His *Fantaisie-Impromptu* is one of his best-known pieces, despite the fact he never wanted it to be published!

## LITERATURE

In 1834, when *Fantaisie-Impromptu* was written, the great Russian poet and author Alexander Pushkin wrote the short story *The Queen of Spades,* a tale of human greed. Composers Tchaikovsky and Franz von Suppé both wrote operas based on Pushkin's story.

## WORLD

In 1834, final modifications were made to the present form of Braille, a system used to help the blind read and write. Fish lovers sent up a cheer when sardines were canned for the first time in Europe.

### 1.9 FANTAISIE-IMPROMPTU

Frédéric Chopin

TRACK 1 15

**Andante**

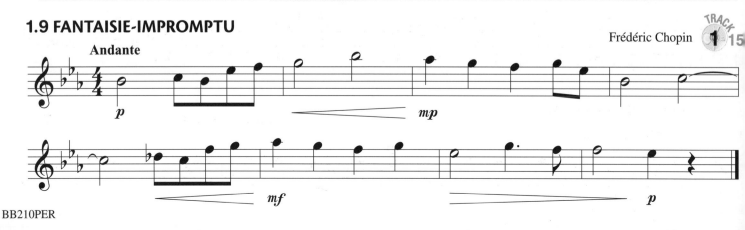

5

## LET'S REVIEW

The following music will help you to remember these important elements:

**Key of A♭ Major** | **Time Signature** 2/4 | **Eighth Rest**

**Tempo Marking** *Moderato* | **Accent** | **Pick-up Note**

### 1.10 THEME FROM SYMPHONY NO. 1 – Duet
Johannes Brahms

### 1.11 ALL NIGHT, ALL DAY
Traditional Spiritual

## HISTORY

### MUSIC
**Jacques Offenbach** (1819–1880) was born in Germany as "Jacob" but became "Jacques" when he moved to Paris to study cello at the Paris Conservatoire. He is best known for his operettas (he wrote almost 100 of them!), including *Orpheus in the Underworld*, which includes the famous *Can-can.*

### LITERATURE
Henry Wadsworth Longfellow wrote the narrative poem *The Courtship of Miles Standish.* Standish was a passenger on the Mayflower and became Plymouth Colony's assistant governor. Just a few years later, Charles Dickens wrote *Great Expectations,* a story of an orphan boy named Pip who faced personal struggles that shaped his life and character.

### WORLD
In 1858, a series of seven debates between Abraham Lincoln and Stephen Douglas were held in Illinois. That year, Minnesota was admitted to the union as the 32nd state. Pencils with attached erasers, as well as rotary washing machines, were patented.

### 1.12 CAN-CAN *Remember to play accents one dynamic louder. Be sure to use correct mallet height.*
Jacques Offenbach

### 1.13 CRIPPLE CREEK
Appalachian Folk Song

### 1.14 THE MARINES' HYMN
Official Song of the U.S. Marine Corps

BB210PER

6

LET'S REVIEW

The following music will help you to remember these important elements:

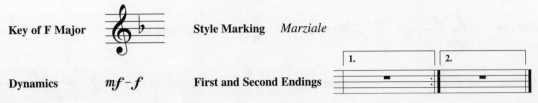

## 1.15 THE MAN ON THE FLYING TRAPEZE

Gaston Lyle

## 1.16 THE CUCKOO WOODPECKER

## 1.17 BACKYARD STOMP

## 1.18 TURKISH MARCH *Remember to change dynamics on the repeat.*

Wolfgang Amadeus Mozart

## 1.19 FLOWER DRUM SONG

Chinese Folk Song

## 1.20 TECHNIQUE TWISTER *Keep a steady beat. Try playing with a metronome!*

BB210PER

## LET'S REVIEW

The following music will help you to remember these important elements:

Chromatics and Accidentals

## 1.21 CHA-CHA CHROMATICA

TRACK 1/27

Allegro

## 1.22 TWO-FACED POLKA

TRACK 1/28

Moderato

*Hey!*

### HISTORY

**MUSIC**

*Hungarian Dance No. 5* comes from a set of 21 dances written by **Johannes Brahms** (1833–1897) and based mostly on Hungarian melodies. Ironically, Brahms accidentally based this piece on a folk dance by another composer, Kéler Béla, thinking that it was a traditional folk song.

**LITERATURE**

Leo Tolstoy wrote his epic novel *War and Peace,* a work of historical fiction that is considered a classic to this day. American novelist Louisa May Alcott, who is best known for writing *Little Women,* published the sequel entitled *Good Wives,* which followed the lives of the *Little Women* as they grew into adulthood.

**WORLD**

In 1869, the Suez Canal opened in Egypt. This man-made waterway connects the Mediterranean and Red Seas. John Willis Menard became the first African-American to speak in Congress in that same year. The Cincinnati Red Stockings became the first professional baseball team in the United States.

## 1.23 HUNGARIAN DANCE NO. 5

Johannes Brahms    TRACK 1/29

Allegro

## 1.24 FINGER TWISTER

TRACK 1/30

# OPUS 1 ENCORE!

## INTERPRETATION STATION

Listen to CD 1 Track 31. You will hear two versions of each example.
Choose the version (A or B) that has better phrasing. Circle your answer.

1. A  B          2. A  B          3. A  B          4. A  B

## SIMON "SEZ"

Listen to CD 1 Track 32. You will hear a well-known musical work. Listen first, sing it, then find the pitches on your instrument.
You can then play along with the accompaniment track that follows. Can you match the notes and style of the recording?

## COMPOSER'S CORNER

Using only the notes from the Concert B♭ Major Scale, complete this composition. Refer to the time signature.
Remember to add dynamics. Give your piece a title and perform it for a friend or family member!

Title:_____          Name:_____

## PENCIL POWER

In Opus 1, you reviewed many of the musical concepts you learned in *Measures of Success* Book 1.
Match each item on the left with its correct term or definition by writing in the appropriate letter.

1. _____ *Marziale*          9. _____ 𝅝‿♩

2. _____ 𝄾          10. _____ ♩

3. _____ 𝄇          11. _____ ,

4. _____ *Andante*          12. _____ 𝄴

5. _____ 𝄐          13. _____ <

6. _____ *Allegro*          14. _____ ♯, ♭

7. _____ *rit.*          15. _____ >  >

8. _____ 𝟤/𝟦          16. _____ ♩.

A. Tenuto                    I. Pick-up Note

B. Walking Tempo            J. Accidental

C. Fast Tempo               K. Accent

D. Gradually Slow Down      L. Eighth Rest

E. Staccato                 M. March Style

F. Gradually Get Louder     N. Breath Mark

G. Fermata                  O. Tie

H. Repeat                   P. Time Signature

## CURTAIN UP!

Time to perform! Play this piece for friends or family members. Remember to introduce the piece by its title and bow when you are finished.

### 1.25 CHESTER

William Billings

# OPUS 2

**NEW NOTE!** **D**

**NEW NOTE!** **C**

**NEW NOTE!** **B♭**

## 2.1 SEPARATION ANXIETY

TRACK 1 · 34

## 2.2 THE GRUMPY PIRATE

Traditional Sea Shanty Melody

TRACK 1 · 35

**Animato** *(animated or lively)*

## 2.3 RUMBA CUBANA! *A rumba is a rhythmic Cuban dance that has Spanish and African origins.*

TRACK 1 · 36

**Energico** *(energetically)*

*Fine*

*D.C. al Fine*

**ON THE PODIUM**

**CONDUCTING REVIEW: 4/4 TIME**

## 2.4 CHICKEN ON A FENCE POST

American Folk Song

TRACK 1 · 37

**ON THE PODIUM**

**Allegro**

# ROLLS ON KEYBOARD PERCUSSION INSTRUMENTS

In order to sustain longer note values on keyboard percussion instruments, it is necessary to roll. All rolls on keyboard percussion instruments are **single stroke rolls.** Play even, steady and consistent primary strokes in the center of the bars. Keep the head of the left mallet above the head of the right mallet.

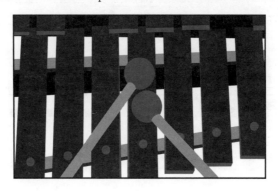

 FOR PERCUSSION ONLY

These exercises are based on your knowledge of sixteenth notes from the front side of your book. If you need some more information on sixteenth notes, turn to Opus 3 on the keyboard percussion side of your book.

As you begin practicing these exercises, start by using a metronome at a **slow tempo.** Play the sixteenth notes evenly with just one hand. Then when the slashes occur, add the other hand exactly in between the steady sixteenth notes. This will sound very similar to the double stroke roll on snare drum but it is produced with single strokes and **no bounces.** Notice that these rolls **begin and end with the same hand.**

Start with your **right hand** when the notes are **moving up** and start with your **left hand** when the notes are **moving down.** For each exercise, practice starting with either hand. Play each exercise in the different keys and scales you have learned. As your rolls develop, gradually increase the tempo on the metronome.

All rolls in this book should be performed on xylophone or marimba unless otherwise notated.

## Exercise 1

## Exercise 2

## Exercise 3

## Exercise 4

## Exercise 5 *Practice various scales using this pattern.*

## Exercise 6 *Remember to start with your right hand when moving up and left hand when moving down.*

10

**HISTORY**

**MUSIC**

**George M. Cohan** (1878–1942), known as "Mr. Broadway", wrote many musicals that were staged on Broadway in New York. His memorable melodies are still loved and sung today. Some of his most notable songs are *Yankee Doodle Dandy, Give My Regards to Broadway,* and *You're a Grand Old Flag,* a song that paid tribute to the U.S. flag and won him a Congressional Gold Medal in 1936.

**LITERATURE**

Eric Arthur Blair, who was better known by his pen name George Orwell, was a British author who made a profound impact on literature. Just after Cohan died, Orwell wrote *Animal Farm,* a story of corruption, greed and ignorance. It is considered to be among the greatest English-language novels ever written.

**WORLD**

In 1906, the world's first animated cartoon was released. In the same year, the first airplane flight in Europe took place in Paris, and the SOS international distress signal was adopted.

## 2.5 YOU'RE A GRAND OLD FLAG  *Circle the ♪♩♪ syncopations!*
*Remember to roll only on xylophone or marimba unless otherwise notated.*

George M. Cohan

TRACK 1 3

## 2.6 SUMMIT FANFARE *Stop the roll just before the end of the measure. Do not play a strong last note - just lift off the bar.*

TRACK 1 3

## 2.7 THE FOREST OWL

Japanese Folk Song

TRACK 1 4

## 2.8 LITTLE BROWN JUG

Joseph E. Winner

TRACK 1 41

BB210PER

## CUT TIME (ALLA BREVE)

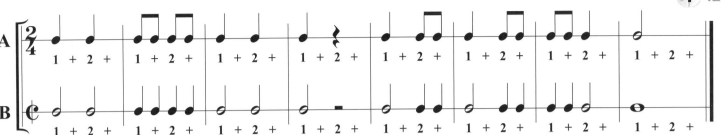

$\math$ = **2 / 2** = **2 / ○** — **2 beats** in each measure. Half note gets one beat.

### 2.9 BEAT STREET – Duet

### 2.10 CUT IT OUT!

**HISTORY**

**MUSIC**

**Modest Mussorgsky** (1839–1881) was a Russian composer whose music has a strong nationalistic flavor. The *Great Gate of Kiev* is the final movement of the larger work *Pictures at an Exhibition,* completed in 1874. It depicts a monumental gate designed for Tsar Alexander II.

**LITERATURE**

In 1874, French author Victor Hugo, who is famous for the novels *Les Misérables* and *The Hunchback of Notre Dame,* wrote *Ninety-Three,* a novel set in 1793 during the French Revolution. Around the same time, William Wells Brown wrote *The Rising Sun.* Brown is considered the first African-American to have published a novel.

**WORLD**

The first zoo in the U.S. opened in 1874 in Philadelphia, PA. Around the same time, P.T. Barnum's Circus (later to become the Barnum and Bailey Circus), the largest in the U.S., made its debut and began traveling the country by railroad.

### 2.11 THE GREAT GATE OF KIEV

Modest Mussorgsky

### 2.12 MANHATTAN BEACH *Play rolls for the full note durations and release each roll on the new pitch.*

John Philip Sousa

12

**THEORY**

## CHORDS

A chord is comprised of three or more pitches played simultaneously. A **major chord** uses the 1st, 3rd, and 5th notes of a major scale. A **minor chord** is created by lowering the 3rd note of the scale one half step.

**THEORY**

## STYLE AND FORM: TRIO

A **trio** has three different parts performed simultaneously by three individuals or groups.

### 2.13 MOOD CHANGE – Trio *Listen to how the B line changes the tonality of the chords from major to minor.*

*Three different percussionists should play these notes. Play smooth, steady and even single stroke rolls. Stay relaxed.*
*The rolls will not stop when you change pitch. Lead with the RH when the pitches go up and the LH when the pitches go down.*

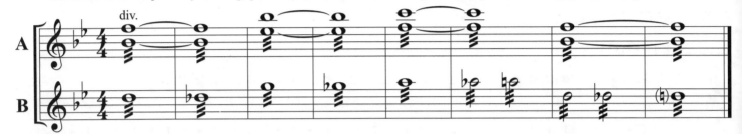

**THEORY**

## NATURAL AND HARMONIC MINOR SCALES

The **natural minor** scale has eight notes going up or down in consecutive order, all in the key signature of the scale name. In your key of G minor, all eight notes are in the key signature of G minor, which has two flats. The **harmonic minor** scale raises the 7th scale note of a natural minor scale by one half step.

**G Natural Minor:**

**G Harmonic Minor:**

## 2.14 CONCERT G NATURAL MINOR SCALE, ARPEGGIO AND CHORD

## 2.15 CONCERT G HARMONIC MINOR SCALE, ARPEGGIO AND CHORD

## 2.16 MINKA

Russian Folk Song

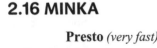

BB210PER

## 2.17 THE DRONING BAGPIPES

TRACK 1 50

### NEW KEY SIGNATURE

This is the key of **C Major**.  This key signature indicates that there are no sharps or flats.

## 2.18 CONCERTO THEME

Ludwig van Beethoven TRACK 1 51

## 2.19 CHEKI, MORENA

Puerto Rican Dance TRACK 1 52

### CUT TIME SYNCOPATION

Remember that weak beats are stressed in syncopation. Look at these examples.
Keeping a steady beat, clap and count the rhythm for each. They sound the same!

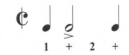

## 2.20 CHEKI, MORENA OTRA VEZ!

Puerto Rican Dance TRACK 1 53

14

**HISTORY**

**MUSIC**

**Camille Saint-Saëns** (1835–1921) was a French composer whose works included symphonic poems, symphonies and operas. *Bacchanale* is from the opera *Samson and Delilah,* completed in 1876. No opera house in France made any effort to stage it until Franz Listz helped arrange the first production a year later.

**LITERATURE**

Anna Sewell's novel *Black Beauty* was published in 1877. It was Sewell's first and only novel. Since its publication, millions of readers have enjoyed this book, a horse's memoir. It has become one of the best-selling books in the world.

**WORLD**

In 1877, Thomas Edison invented the Edisonphone, a tin cylinder phonograph that made the first recording. Also in 1877, the oldest tennis tournament in the world, Wimbledon, held its first men's tennis match.

## 2.21 BACCHANALE FROM SAMSON AND DELILAH

*Notice the counting in measure 11 for the dotted half note.*

Camille Saint-Saëns

## 2.22 CHROMAT-ATTACK (FIGHT SONG) – Duet

**THEORY**

## IMPROVISATION

**Improvisation** occurs when performers compose and play music
on the spot, without rehearsal and without reading notation.

## 2.23 KLEZMER! – Improvisation

*Use the guide notes to improvise while a partner plays the music below,
or play along with the CD. (Note: The CD recording repeats 4 times.)*

# OPUS 2 ENCORE!

## INTERPRETATION STATION

Listen to CD 1 Track 57. You will hear pairs of chords or scales. Listen to each pair, comparing the second example to the first. Decide if the second example in each pair is Major or minor. Circle your answers.

**1.** Major minor     **2.** Major minor     **3.** Major minor     **4.** Major minor

## SIMON "SEZ"

Listen to CD 1 Track 58. You will hear a well-known musical work. Listen first, sing it, then find the pitches on your instrument. You can then play along with the accompaniment track that follows. Can you match the notes and style of the recording?

## COMPOSER'S CORNER

Using your knowledge of Major and minor, transform *London Bridge* into *Lonely Bridge* by rewriting it in a minor key. Think about which notes will need accidentals. The first two measures have already been completed for you!

### LONDON BRIDGE
Traditional

### LONELY BRIDGE

## PENCIL POWER – CREATING MAJOR AND MINOR CHORDS

Decide if the chord is Major or minor. Circle your answer. Be careful! Example 5 is tricky!

**1.** Major minor    **2.** Major minor    **3.** Major minor    **4.** Major minor    **5.** Major minor

Correctly add notes to create the chord. Be careful! Example 10 is tricky!

**6.** E♭ Major    **7.** C Major    **8.** B♭ minor    **9.** A♭ Major    **10.** E♭ minor

## SIGHT READING

Sight reading is a way to demonstrate what you know about reading and performing music. Remember the **Three Ps** to help you sight read:

    **Preview:** Title, composer, key signature, time signature, tempo, style, articulation and expression markings
    **Process:** Imagine the flow of the music, silently sticking through transitions and complex passages
    **Perform:** Set your posture and grip, then play the passage as musically as possible

### 2.24 ELEMENTS – Sight Reading

# CURTAIN UP!

## 2.25 MARCHE MILITAIRE

Franz Schubert
arr. Robert Sheldon

## 2.26 SUNSET ON THE CHESAPEAKE

Brian Balmages

# ✳ OPUS 3

**SIXTEENTH NOTES**

Sixteenth Note = quarter beat of sound

Beamed Sixteenth Notes

1 e + a

**3.1 BEAT STREET** *Tap your foot to keep a steady beat!*

Begin CD 2  TRACK 2 1

1 e + a 2 e + a    1 e + a 2 e + a    1 e + a 2 e + a    1 e + a 2 e + a

**3.2 SWEET SIXTEEN**

TRACK 2 2

1 e + a 2 e + a    1 e + a 2 e + a    1 e + a 2 e + a    1 e + a 2 e + a

**3.3 TSAR NIKOLAI**

Russian Folk Song  TRACK 2 3

Andante

*mf*

**3.4 CARIBBEAN HOLIDAY**

TRACK 2 4

Calypso

*Fine*

*f*

*D.C. al Fine*

*mp*

*f*

**3.5 THE THUNDERER** *Notice how eighth notes are counted in cut time.*

John Philip Sousa  TRACK 2 5

March tempo

*f*

2 e + a    2 e + a

**1.**

**2.**

2 e + a

BB210PER

## EIGHTH NOTE/TWO SIXTEENTH NOTE GROUP

An eighth note can replace the first two sixteenth notes in a group of four sixteenth notes.
This creates an **eighth note/two sixteenth note group.**

1 (e) + a        1 (e) + a

### 3.6 BEAT STREET

1 e + a 2 e + a        1 e + a 2 e + a        1 e + a 2 e + a        1 e + a 2 e + a

### 3.7 16TH STREET

1 e + a 2 e + a        1 e + a 2 e + a        1 e + a 2 e + a        1 e + a 2 e + a

## ONE-MEASURE REPEAT

%        Repeat the preceding measure.

### 3.8 THE KING'S TRUMPETERS – Duet

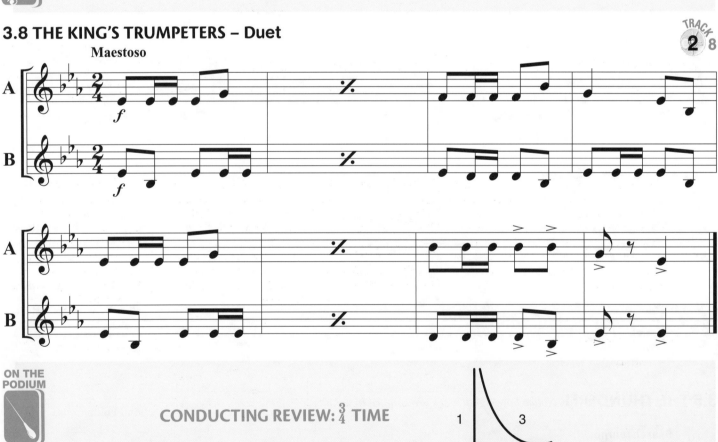

## CONDUCTING REVIEW: $\frac{3}{4}$ TIME

1        3

2

### 3.9 THE MATADOR

## HISTORY

### MUSIC

*Trepak,* based on a Ukrainian folk dance, is part of the famous ballet *The Nutcracker,* written by **Pyotr I. Tchaikovsky** (1840–1893). Based on Hoffman's *The Nutcracker and the Mouse King,* it remains a favorite among listeners, especially during the holidays.

### LITERATURE

Scottish author Robert Louis Stevenson introduced the world to the fictitious pirate, Long John Silver, in his novel, *Treasure Island.* This adventure tells the tale of pirates and buried gold. Also, J.R.R. Tolkien, author of *The Hobbit* and *Lord of the Rings,* was born the same year *The Nutcracker* was premiered.

### WORLD

In 1892, Ellis Island became the official welcome center for immigrants to the U.S., Fig Newtons® were first produced and to make sure you had a sparkling smile after you ate them, the toothpaste tube was invented!

## 3.10 TREPAK

Pytor I. Tchaikovsky

TRACK **2** 10

## 3.11 OLD JOE CLARK

American Folk Song

TRACK **2** 11

**NEW NOTE!**
**D♭**

## HISTORY

### MUSIC

*Green Bushes* is an English folk song that has been used by several composers. **Percy Grainger** (1882–1961) was a composer born in Australia who wrote some of the most notable works in the wind band literature. He used *Green Bushes* in several of his works including *Lincolnshire Posy* and *Green Bushes (Passacaglia on an English Folksong).*

### LITERATURE

The children's novel *A Little Princess* was written by Frances Hodgson Burnett. American author Jack London wrote his most famous novel, *The Call of the Wild,* a story about a domesticated dog that eventually turns back into a wild animal. London soon followed with a companion novel, *White Fang.*

### WORLD

Around the turn of the century, the Canadian provinces of Saskatchewan and Alberta were established. Front-wheel drive for automobiles was patented by a German engineer, and Las Vegas officially became a city in the U.S.

## 3.12 GREEN BUSHES

English Folk Song

TRACK **2** 12

BB210PER

## TWO SIXTEENTH NOTE/EIGHTH NOTE GROUP

An eighth note can replace the last two sixteenth notes in a group of four sixteenth notes. This creates a **two sixteenth note/eighth note group.**

### 3.13 BEAT STREET

### 3.14 ANOTHER WAY

### 3.15 STODOLA PUMPA
Moderato

Czech Folk Song

### 3.16 LA MORISQUE
Maestoso

Tielman Susato

### 3.17 SKYWARD
Allegro

### 3.18 THE MOREEN
Allegro

Irish Air

## CONDUCTING REVIEW: 2/4 TIME

### 3.19 JIM ALONG JOSEY
Animato

American Folk Song

## 3.20 SQUARE DANCE – Duet

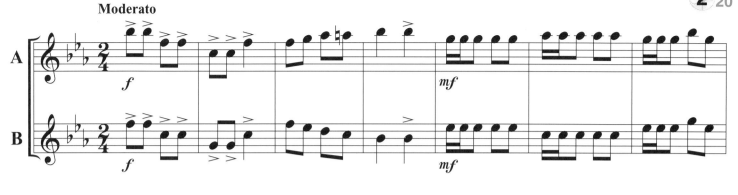

## KEY CHANGE

A **key change** occurs when music moves from one key to another in a single musical work. You will know a key change has occurred when you see a double bar line followed by a new key signature. The new key signature shows the new sharps or flats and may also contain natural signs that cancel the sharps or flats from the previous key signature.

## 3.21 CHANGE UP (CONCERT F TO B♭ MAJOR)

## 3.22 DECK THE HALLS  *What is the starting key signature?*  *What is the ending key signature?*          Welsh Carol

22

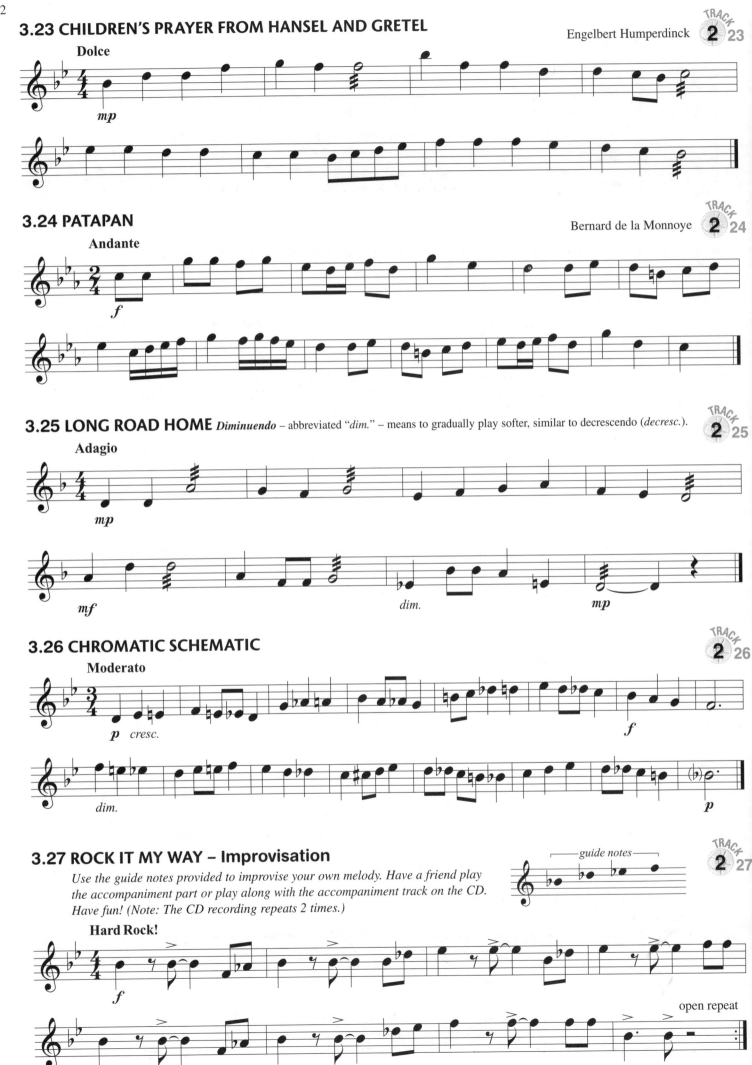

### 3.23 CHILDREN'S PRAYER FROM HANSEL AND GRETEL

Engelbert Humperdinck

**Dolce**

*mp*

### 3.24 PATAPAN

Bernard de la Monnoye

**Andante**

*f*

### 3.25 LONG ROAD HOME
*Diminuendo* – abbreviated "*dim.*" – means to gradually play softer, similar to decrescendo (*decresc.*).

**Adagio**

*mp*

*mf*

*dim.*

*mp*

### 3.26 CHROMATIC SCHEMATIC

**Moderato**

*p* *cresc.*

*f*

*dim.*

*p*

### 3.27 ROCK IT MY WAY – Improvisation

*Use the guide notes provided to improvise your own melody. Have a friend play the accompaniment part or play along with the accompaniment track on the CD. Have fun! (Note: The CD recording repeats 2 times.)*

guide notes

**Hard Rock!**

*f*

open repeat

# OPUS 3 ENCORE!

## INTERPRETATION STATION

Listen to CD 2 Track 28. You will hear a tempo given by a click track. This is the speed of the quarter note. After each click track you will hear a rhythm. Select which notated rhythm is being played and write the corresponding answer letter on the line. Each example is performed twice.

1. _____    3. _____

2. _____    4. _____

## SIMON "SEZ"

Listen to CD 2 Track 29. You will hear a well-known musical work. Listen first, sing it, then find the pitches on your instrument. You can then play along with the accompaniment track that follows. Can you match the notes and style of the recording?

## COMPOSER'S CORNER

Many composers use key changes as a compositional technique. Rewrite this melody in the key of Concert E♭ Major. Then play the entire piece!

### SWEETLY SINGS THE DONKEY

Traditional

## PENCIL POWER

Rewrite the following musical examples in either 2/4 or cut time. Pay attention to how you beam eighth notes and sixteenth notes!

## SIGHT READING

Remember the Three Ps to help you sight read: **Preview, Process, Perform.**

### 3.28 LINE OF SIGHT – Sight Reading

Moderato

*mf*

*p*

*mf*

*f*

# CURTAIN UP!

## 3.29 BARN DANCE

Brian Balmages

TRACK 2 / 31

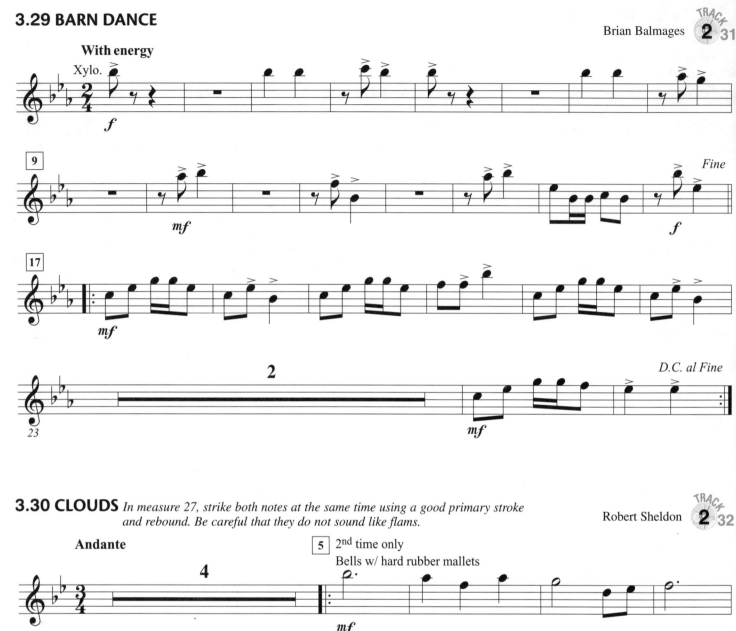

## 3.30 CLOUDS
*In measure 27, strike both notes at the same time using a good primary stroke and rebound. Be careful that they do not sound like flams.*

Robert Sheldon

TRACK 2 / 32

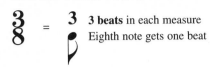

## 4.5 PARADE OF THE WOODEN SOLDIERS – Duet

Leon Jessel

## 4.6 WACKY WALTZ

NEW NOTE!
F#/Gb

Andante

### RALLENTANDO

**Rallentando** – abbreviated "*rall.*" – means to gradually slow down, similar to ritardando (*rit.*).

## 4.7 DARK OVERTURE

Adagio

## 4.8 TAFTA HINDI

Arabic Folk Song

Moderato

## 4.9 À LA BAROQUE

Andante

## 4.10 THE RAKES OF MALLOW

Irish Folk Song

Allegretto

## D.C. AL CODA

Remember that D.C. is an abbreviation for *da capo,* an Italian term that refers to the beginning. A **coda** contains music that occurs at the end of a piece. **D.C. al Coda** means to return to the beginning and play until you come to the **coda sign,** ⊕. When you see the coda sign, skip to ⊕ **Coda** and play to the end.

## 4.11 GIVE MY REGARDS TO BROADWAY *Be sure to observe all the signs!*

George M. Cohan

*In cut time, be careful not to roll too fast. The roll speed will be based on eighth notes.*

## 4.12 IN A FUNK *Funk has roots in rhythm and blues. It was developed in the 1960s and 1970s and features strong bass lines.*

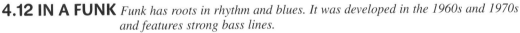

## 4.13 ROUGH WATERS

Andantino *(slightly faster than Andante)*

BB210PER

## MORE TIME SIGNATURES

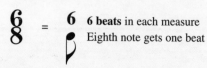

$\frac{6}{8}$ = **6** **6 beats** in each measure
♪ Eighth note gets one beat

In a faster tempo, emphasis is often placed on the 1st and 4th beats of each measure.
This gives the music a strong 2-beat pulse.

### 4.14 BEAT STREET

TRACK **2** 4

### 4.15 ROYAL FANFARE

TRACK **2** 4

**Maestoso**

### 4.16 LOOBY LOO *Conduct using a 2-beat pattern.*

Traditional   TRACK **2** 48

ON THE PODIUM

**Moderato**

### 4.17 UN CANADIEN ERRANT

French-Canadian Folk Song   TRACK **2** 49

**Andantino**

### 4.18 THE KERRY DANCE

Irish Folk Song   TRACK **2** 50

**Moderato**

## 4.19 WALLABY STEW

Australian Folk Song

TRACK 2 51

**Allegretto**

*mf*

## 4.20 GRADUAL ASCENT

TRACK 2 52

**NEW NOTE!** Ab

Ab

### HISTORY

#### MUSIC
**Bedřich Smetana** (1824–1884) was a musical hero to the Czech people. He wrote music with a very strong nationalistic flavor. *The Moldau,* premiered in 1875, is a movement of his larger work *Má vlast (My Motherland).* It represents the beauty and strength of the great Bohemian Moldau river.

#### LITERATURE
American poet and master of the macabre Edgar Allan Poe, who died in 1849, was exhumed and reburied in 1875 in order to dedicate a grave marker to him. Almost fittingly, controversy still exists on whether or not the right body was reburied.

#### WORLD
In 1875, the English Channel was conquered by swimmer Matthew Webb. Folks with tummy troubles had new relief as Phillips'® Milk of Magnesia was introduced (it is still available in drug stores today!).

## 4.21 THEME FROM THE MOLDAU – Duet

Bedřich Smetana

TRACK 2 53

**Andante**

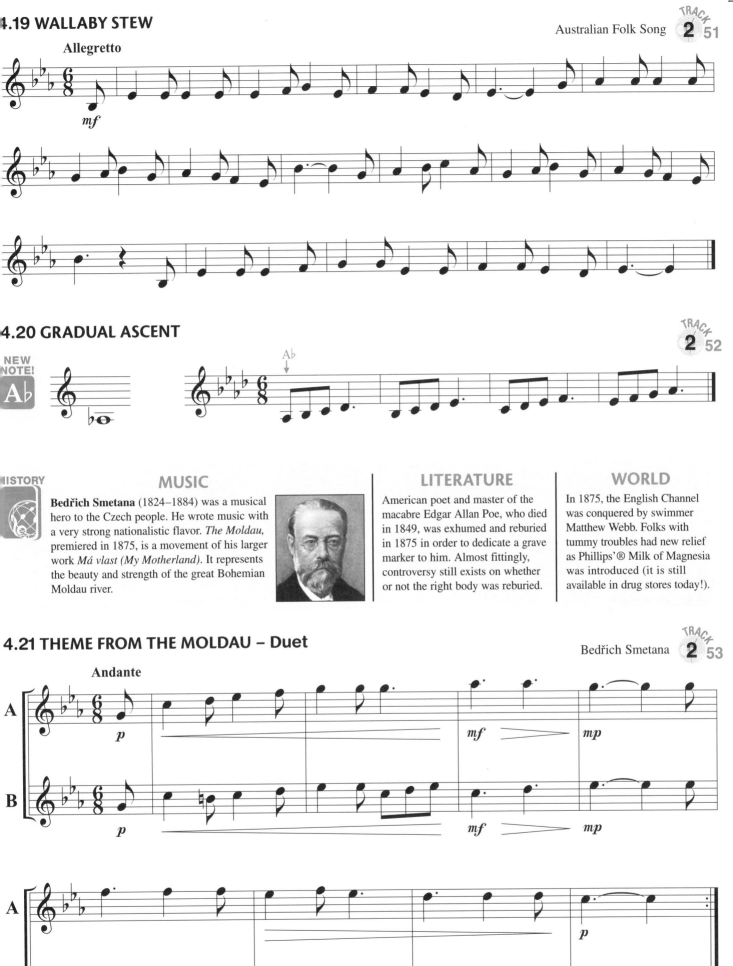

BB210PER

**RHYTHM**

## DOTTED EIGHTH NOTE/SIXTEENTH NOTE GROUP

Adding a dot after a note increases the length of the note by half of its value.
Here the dot is used with an eighth note to create a **dotted eighth note.**

### 4.22 BEAT STREET – Duet

TRACK **2** 54

### 4.23 REGIMENT – Duet

TRACK **2** 55

### 4.24 COUNTRY GARDENS

English Folk Song

TRACK **2** 56

**ON THE PODIUM**

**THEORY**

## A TEMPO

The term **a tempo** means to return to the previous tempo.

### 4.25 LA DONNA È MOBILE *Keep steady strokes in the roll on the fermata.*
*Be sure to stop the roll with a lift on the cut off.*

Giuseppe Verdi

TRACK **2** 57

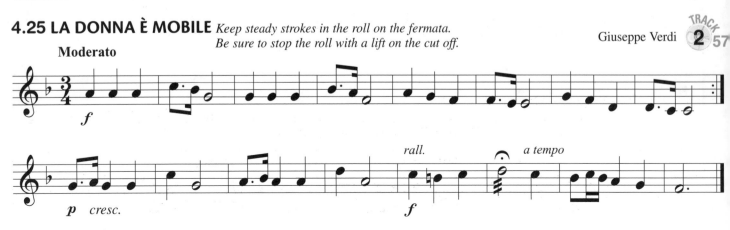

**HISTORY**

## MUSIC

**Richard Wagner** (1813–1883) was a German composer who wrote music noted for its rich harmonies and thick textures. Wagner's opera *Lohengrin*, first performed in 1850, contains the well-known *Wedding March* which is still a popular processional at many weddings.

## LITERATURE

Poet Alfred Lord Tennyson became the United Kingdom's Poet Laureate in 1850. A high honor, the Poet Laureate is an official appointment bestowed by the government on a poet of great stature, who is called upon to write poems that commemorate important national events. In the U.S., American abolitionist and author Harriet Beecher Stowe wrote *Uncle Tom's Cabin*, sparking a national debate on slavery.

## WORLD

In 1850, Australia's oldest university, the University of Sydney, was founded. At the same time, Harriet Tubman was deemed the official conductor of the Underground Railroad.

## 4.26 BRIDAL CHORUS FROM LOHENGRIN

Richard Wagner

**HISTORY**

## MUSIC

**Franz Schubert** (1797–1828) had only completed two movements of his *Symphony No. 8 ("Unfinished")* before he left it for good. Other composers have offered versions of the complete symphony. No one really knows why Schubert did not finish the work. It is a musical mystery!

## LITERATURE

Scottish author Sir Walter Scott wrote *Ivanhoe*, a novel in which Robin Hood made his first appearance. The story helped shape the modern concept of him as a cheerful, noble outlaw. At the same time, Catharine Sedgwick was writing novels and short stories in the United States. She was a champion of Republican motherhood, believing that mothers had a civic duty to raise children to be model citizens.

## WORLD

In 1822, the United States officially recognized Mexico as an autonomous country. Dinosaur fossils and skeletons were discovered on the east coast of the U.S.

## 4.27 THEME FROM SYMPHONY NO. 8

Franz Schubert

## 4.28 TARANTELLA

Italian Folk Song

## 4.29 CHANT – Improvisation

*Use the guide notes to improvise while a partner plays the music below, or play along with the CD. (Note: The CD recording repeats 4 times.)*

BB210PER

## INTERPRETATION STATION

TRACK **2** 62

Listen to CD 2 Track 62. For each example, determine the time signature. Circle your answer.

1. $\frac{2}{4}$ $\frac{3}{8}$     2. $\frac{6}{8}$ $\frac{4}{4}$     3. $\frac{3}{4}$ $\mathbb{C}$     4. $\mathbb{C}$ $\frac{3}{8}$

## SIMON "SEZ"

TRACK **2** 63

Listen to CD 2 Track 63. You will hear a well-known musical work. Listen first, sing it, then find the pitches on your instrument.
You can then play along with the accompaniment track that follows. Can you match the notes and style of the recording?

## COMPOSER'S CORNER

Write a melody for this duet using the guide notes provided. Pair up with a friend and perform it for your class or family!

Choose from these guide notes:

Title: _____     Composer: _____

## PENCIL POWER

Match each definition with its correct term or symbol by writing in the appropriate letter.

1. _____ Two beats in each measure; half note gets one beat
2. _____ Three or more pitches sounding simultaneously
3. _____ Three different parts performed simultaneously by three different individuals or groups
4. _____ Merry
5. _____ Playing music on the spot without rehearsal or notation
6. _____ Three beats in each measure; eighth note gets one beat
7. _____ Slightly slower than *Allegro*
8. _____ Coda
9. _____ Faster than *Allegro*
10. _____ Animated or lively

A. Animato
B. Presto
C. ⊕
D. Giocoso
E. $\frac{3}{8}$
F. Trio
G. Allegretto
H. $\mathbb{C}$
I. Chord
J. Improvisation

## SIGHT READING

Remember the Three Ps to help you sight read: **Preview, Process, Perform.**

## 4.30 DANZA – Sight Reading

TRACK **2** 64

**Moderato**

33

# CURTAIN UP!

**FULL BAND**

**4.31 GARRYOWEN** *The jig, a popular dance originating in Ireland and Scotland, has a variety of repeated motions and is often set in 6/8 time.*

Irish Folk Song
arr. Robert Sheldon

TRACK 2 65

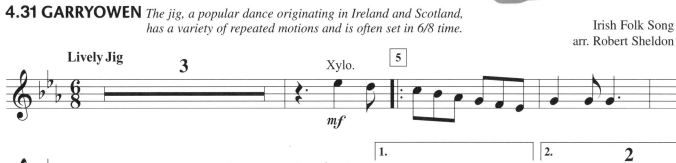

**4.32 AMERICA, THE BEAUTIFUL** *Molto is an Italian term that means "very much."*

Samuel A. Ward
arr. Brian Balmages

TRACK 2 66

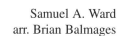 

BB210PER

# OPUS 5

## 5.1 TOP OF THE MORNING

**Moderato**

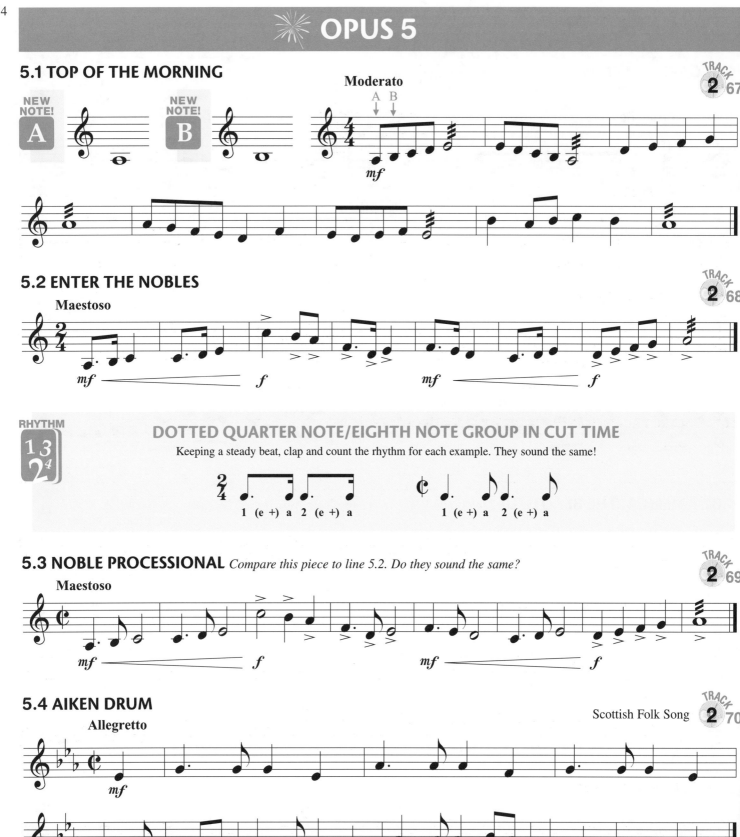

## 5.2 ENTER THE NOBLES

**Maestoso**

### DOTTED QUARTER NOTE/EIGHTH NOTE GROUP IN CUT TIME

Keeping a steady beat, clap and count the rhythm for each example. They sound the same!

## 5.3 NOBLE PROCESSIONAL *Compare this piece to line 5.2. Do they sound the same?*

**Maestoso**

## 5.4 AIKEN DRUM

Scottish Folk Song

**Allegretto**

## 5.5 BLOW THE MAN DOWN

Sea Shanty

**ON THE PODIUM**

**Moderato**

**RHYTHM 13**

## EIGHTH NOTE TRIPLETS

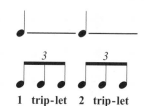

### 5.6 BEAT STREET

Begin CD 3 — TRACK 3·1

### 5.7 TRIPLET FANFARE

TRACK 3·2

### 5.8 FINALE FROM THE NEW WORLD SYMPHONY

Antonín Dvořák — TRACK 3·3

Pesante

### 5.9 LIGHT CAVALRY OVERTURE

Franz von Suppé — TRACK 3·4

Maestoso

### 5.10 STRIVE FOR FIVE

TRACK 3·5

### 5.11 MOLLY MALONE

Irish Folk Song — TRACK 3·6

Andantino

BB210PER

36

**HISTORY**

## MUSIC

**Antonio Vivaldi** (1678–1741) was a composer of the Baroque style. He was a highly skilled violinist and spent most of his life in Venice, Italy. *Autumn* is from a set of violin concertos entitled *The Four Seasons*. It was published in 1725. Vivaldi wrote each movement to be reminiscent of each season of the year.

## LITERATURE

Jonathan Swift was an Irish writer who was known as a master of satire. His novel *Gulliver's Travels* became incredibly popular as soon as it was published and continues to be one of his best-known works.

## WORLD

In 1723, Maryland required the establishment of public schools in all counties. A few years later across the Atlantic Ocean, France suffered from a famine and workers rioted when the price of bread was raised substantially. The coffeehouse craze was in full force in London, which had almost 2,000 of them!

## 5.12 AUTUMN FROM THE FOUR SEASONS

Antonio Vivaldi

**THEORY**

## D.S. AL CODA

D.S. is an abbreviation for the Italian term *dal segno* or the sign, 𝄋. **D.S. al Coda** means to return to the sign (𝄋) and play until you come to the coda sign, 𝄌. When you see the coda sign, skip to the coda and play to the end.

## 5.13 DOWN BY THE STATION *Be sure to observe all the signs!*

American Folk Song

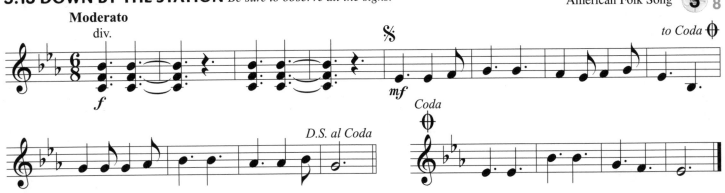

**HISTORY**

## MUSIC

**Johann Strauss I** (1804–1849) was an Austrian composer whose legacy included many waltzes and the famous *Radetzky March,* which became quite popular among soldiers at the time. When Austrian officers first heard it, they clapped along with the chorus. This tradition is still carried on today.

## LITERATURE

Alexandre Dumas, one of France's most renowned writers, wrote *The Queen's Necklace* in 1848. Dumas' most recognizable tales are *The Count of Monte Cristo* and *The Three Musketeers,* the latter telling of a young man named d'Artagnan who leaves home to become a guard of the musketeers.

## WORLD

In 1848, the saxophone was patented, Spain opened its first railroad, and the first Women's Rights convention was held in New York.

## 5.14 RADETZKY MARCH

Johann Strauss I

BB210PER

## 5.15 MARCH CHROMATICA

TRACK 3 10

Marziale

**RHYTHM 13**

## DOTTED QUARTER NOTE/TWO SIXTEENTH NOTE GROUP

## 5.16 BEAT STREET

TRACK 3 11

## 5.17 CHANGING OF THE GUARD

TRACK 3 12

## 5.18 OH! SUSANNA

Stephen C. Foster

TRACK 3 13

Moderato

## 5.19 FINALE FROM SYMPHONY NO. 5

Pyotr I. Tchaikovsky

TRACK 3 14

Maestoso

38

## 5.20 AN AUSTRIAN WENT YODELING

Austrian Folk Song

TRACK 3 - 15

**Allegretto**

## 5.21 MARYBOROUGH MINER *Keep an even roll speed through the crescendo in measure 8.*

Australian Folk Song

TRACK 3 - 16

**Cantabile**

## 5.22 SHABBAT SHALOM

Israeli Folk Song

TRACK 3 - 17

ON THE PODIUM

**Presto**

## 5.23 BATTLE HYMN OF THE REPUBLIC

Traditional American Melody

TRACK 3 - 18

**Stately**

## 5.24 BLUES ROCK – Improvisation

The guide notes provided form a blues scale. Play the notes moving up and down a few times. Then use the notes to improvise your own melody. Have a friend play the accompaniment part or play along with the accompaniment track on the CD. Have fun! (Note: The CD recording repeats 3 times.)

guide notes

TRACK 3 - 19

**Rock**

open repeat

# OPUS 5 ENCORE!

## INTERPRETATION STATION

Listen to CD 3 Track 20. Each example uses one of the musical elements below. Write the corresponding letter in the space provided.

1. _____          2. _____          3. _____          4. _____

**A.** Diminuendo     **B.** Molto ritardando     **C.** Eighth note triplets     **D.** Sixteenth notes

## SIMON "SEZ"

Listen to CD 3 Track 21. You will hear a well-known musical work. Listen first, sing it, then find the pitches on your instrument.
You can then play along with the accompaniment track that follows. Can you match the notes and style of the recording?

## COMPOSER'S CORNER

A fanfare is a short musical flourish usually used for processions or grand entrances. Write a fanfare for your instrument in the key of Concert A♭ Major.
Use at least two sets of eighth note triplets in your music. Title your piece and perform it for family and friends. *Hint: Don't forget the D.S. al Coda!*

Title: _____          Composer: _____

## PENCIL POWER

Study each example and decide its time signature. Write the time signature in the appropriate place on the staff.

1.

3.

**2.** *Two time signatures will work for this example. Use both.*

**4.** *Bonus: This example uses a time signature that you have never seen. Can you figure it out?*

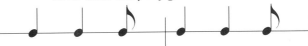

## SIGHT READING

Remember the Three Ps to help you sight read: **Preview, Process, Perform.**

### 5.25 INTRADA – Sight Reading

# CURTAIN UP!

**5.26 TURKISH MARCH FROM THE RUINS OF ATHENS**

Ludwig van Beethoven
arr. Brian Balmages

**5.27 CIRCUS DAZE**

Robert Sheldon

# OPUS 6

**RHYTHM 13**

## METER CHANGES

You have already played pieces with variations that use a meter change.
Sometimes the meter can change within the main melody. Remember these hints:

- Look ahead as you play.
- Check the bottom number of each time signature to determine what kind of note gets one beat.
- Watch your conductor!

### 6.1 PROMENADE FROM PICTURES AT AN EXHIBITION *Bonus: Conduct this piece!* — Modest Mussorgsky — TRACK 3/25

### 6.2 FUM, FUM, FUM — Spanish Carol — TRACK 3/26

### 6.3 SHENANDOAH — American Folk Song — TRACK 3/27

### 6.4 SLITHERY SNAKE — TRACK 3/28

### 6.5 NIGHT ON BALD MOUNTAIN — Modest Mussorgsky — TRACK 3/29

BB210PER

42

## 6.6 MARCH OF THE TOREADORS

Georges Bizet

## 6.7 O TANNENBAUM

German Folk Song

## 6.8 MOUNTAIN CLIMBING

## 6.9 THE BRITISH GRENADIERS

English Marching Song

**HISTORY**

**MUSIC**
English composer **Sir Edward Elgar** (1857–1934) was one of the first composers to take advantage of new technology by recording many of his works to phonograph discs in the early 1900s. His famous march *Pomp and Circumstance* was premiered in 1901 and is often heard at graduation ceremonies.

**LITERATURE**
In 1901, American naturalist John Muir published *Our National Parks,* a collection of essays that helped conservation advocacy. *The Tale of Peter Rabbit* was privately published by Beatrix Potter. It was so successful that a publishing company accepted it a year later.

**WORLD**
British engineer Hubert Booth invented and patented a horse-drawn, house-to-house vacuum cleaner. William S. Harley created a drawing of an engine designed to fit a bicycle. This would be the prototype of the first Harley motorcycle.

## 6.10 POMP AND CIRCUMSTANCE *Remember to keep an even roll speed through the crescendo.* Sir Edward Elgar

BB210PER

## 6.11 MARCH FROM THE NUTCRACKER

Pytor I. Tchaikovsky

## 6.12 WHEN JOHNNY COMES MARCHING HOME

American Folk Song

### HISTORY

#### MUSIC

*Blow Away the Morning Dew* (also known as *The Baffled Knight*) is an English folk song dating back to the early 1600s. British composer **Ralph Vaughan Williams** (1872–1958) used it as one of the main melodies in the third movement of *English Folk Song Suite,* which he wrote for military band in 1923.

#### LITERATURE

In 1911, English playwright and author Frances Hodgson Burnett published *The Secret Garden,* which has become a classic of children's literature. In 1923, Austrian author Felix Salten wrote the novel *Bambi, A Life in the Woods.* This went on to become a successful Disney animated feature.

#### WORLD

*Time* magazine was first published in 1923. It was a big year for candy lovers. Reese's® Peanut Butter Cups, Butterfinger®, and Milky Way® bars were all invented!

## 6.13 BLOW AWAY THE MORNING DEW

English Folk Song

44

| MUSIC | LITERATURE | WORLD |
|---|---|---|
| **Nikolai Rimsky-Korsakov** (1844–1908) was a Russian composer who was also a master of orchestration. *Procession of the Nobles* is from the opera *Mlada,* which had a score that was divided between several composers. The entire project was never completed, yet this remains a popular work. | American author Stephen Crane wrote the war novel *The Red Badge of Courage* in 1895. The story illustrates the harshness of the American Civil War and has become one of the most influential works in American literature. Ironically, Crane was not born until after the war ended. | In 1895, Caroline Willard Baldwin became the first woman to earn a doctor of science degree at Cornell University. Around the same time, William Wrigley Jr. introduced Juicy Fruit® and Wrigley's Spearmint® chewing gum. |

## 6.14 PROCESSION OF THE NOBLES

Nikolai Rimsky-Korsakov

**Pomposo** *(grand and dignified)*

## 6.15 THE STAR-SPANGLED BANNER

U.S. National Anthem

**Stately**

## 6.16 "FINISHED THE BOOK" BLUES – Improvisation

*As in Opus 5, the guide notes provided form a blues scale.*
*The accompaniment part is an example of a "walking bass line,"*
*which is common in swing. Have a friend play the accompaniment part,*
*or play along with the accompaniment track on the CD. Have fun! (Note: The CD recording repeats 2 times.)*

**Swing**

# OPUS 6 ENCORE!

## INTERPRETATION STATION

**TRACK 3 41**

Listen to CD 3 Track 41. For each example, decide which term best fits the music. Circle your answer.

| | | | |
|---|---|---|---|
| **1.** Espressivo | **2.** Pesante | **3.** Marziale | **4.** Giocoso |
| Maestoso | Andantino | Legato | Cantabile |

## SIMON "SEZ"

**TRACK 3 42**

Listen to CD 3 Track 42. You will hear a well-known musical work. Listen first, sing it, and then find the pitches on your instrument. You can then play along with the accompaniment track that follows. Can you match the notes and style of the recording?

## COMPOSER'S CORNER

Write a melody in the key of Concert G minor. Make sure that you have the correct number of beats in each measure by paying attention to the meter changes. Don't forget to add dynamics and articulations. Title your piece and perform it for family and friends.

Title: _____     Composer: _____

## PENCIL POWER – MATCH THE COMPOSER

Match each composition with its composer by writing in the appropriate letter. Be careful! There are more composers than there are compositions!

**1.** _____ Trepak

**2.** _____ Bacchanale from Samson and Delilah

**3.** _____ La Donna è Mobile

**4.** _____ Pomp and Circumstance

**5.** _____ Hungarian Dance No. 5

**6.** _____ Procession of the Nobles

**7.** _____ The Great Gate of Kiev

**8.** _____ The Moldau

**9.** _____ Bridal Chorus from Lohengrin

**10.** _____ Give My Regards to Broadway

| | |
|---|---|
| **A.** Elgar | **G.** Cohan |
| **B.** Mussorgsky | **H.** Rimsky-Korsakov |
| **C.** Wagner | **I.** Tchaikovsky |
| **D.** Smetana | **J.** Brahms |
| **E.** Saint-Saëns | **K.** Verdi |
| **F.** Offenbach | **L.** Strauss |

## SIGHT READING

Remember the Three Ps to help you sight read: **Preview, Process, Perform.**

### 6.17 CHANGES – Sight Reading

**TRACK 3 43**

# CURTAIN UP!

**6.18 ZIMBABWE!**

Robert Sheldon

BB210PER

# 6.19 FIREBOLT FANFARE

Brian Balmages

TRACK **3** 45

BB210PER

## 6.20 TWO DANCES FROM TERPSICHORE
**Instrumental Solo**

### I. BALLET DE GRENOVILLE

Michael Praetorius
arr. Brian Balmages

### II. LA BOUREE

# 6.20 TWO DANCES FROM TERPSICHORE

**Piano Accompaniment**

Michael Praetorius
arr. Brian Balmages

## I. BALLET DE GRENOVILLE

## II. LA BOUREE

BB210PER

# SCALES AND ARPEGGIOS

## CONCERT B♭ MAJOR AND RELATIVE MINOR

**CONCERT B♭ MAJOR**

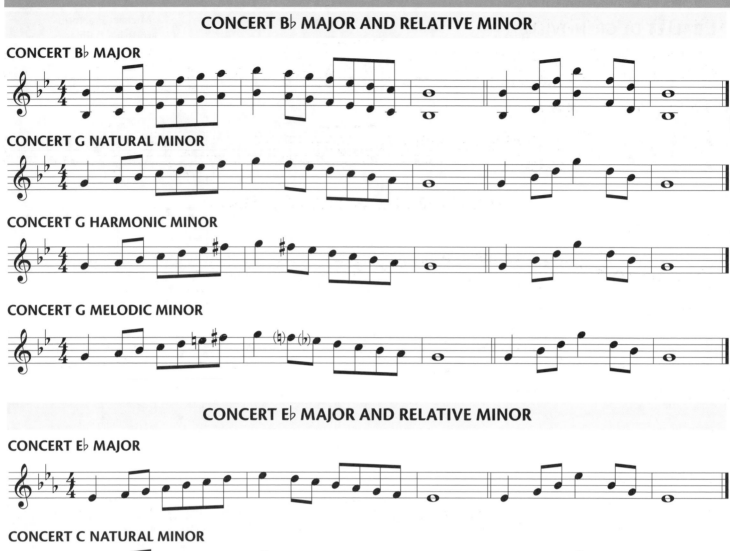

**CONCERT G NATURAL MINOR**

**CONCERT G HARMONIC MINOR**

**CONCERT G MELODIC MINOR**

## CONCERT E♭ MAJOR AND RELATIVE MINOR

**CONCERT E♭ MAJOR**

**CONCERT C NATURAL MINOR**

**CONCERT C HARMONIC MINOR**

**CONCERT C MELODIC MINOR**

## CONCERT A♭ MAJOR AND RELATIVE MINOR

**CONCERT A♭ MAJOR**

**CONCERT F NATURAL MINOR**

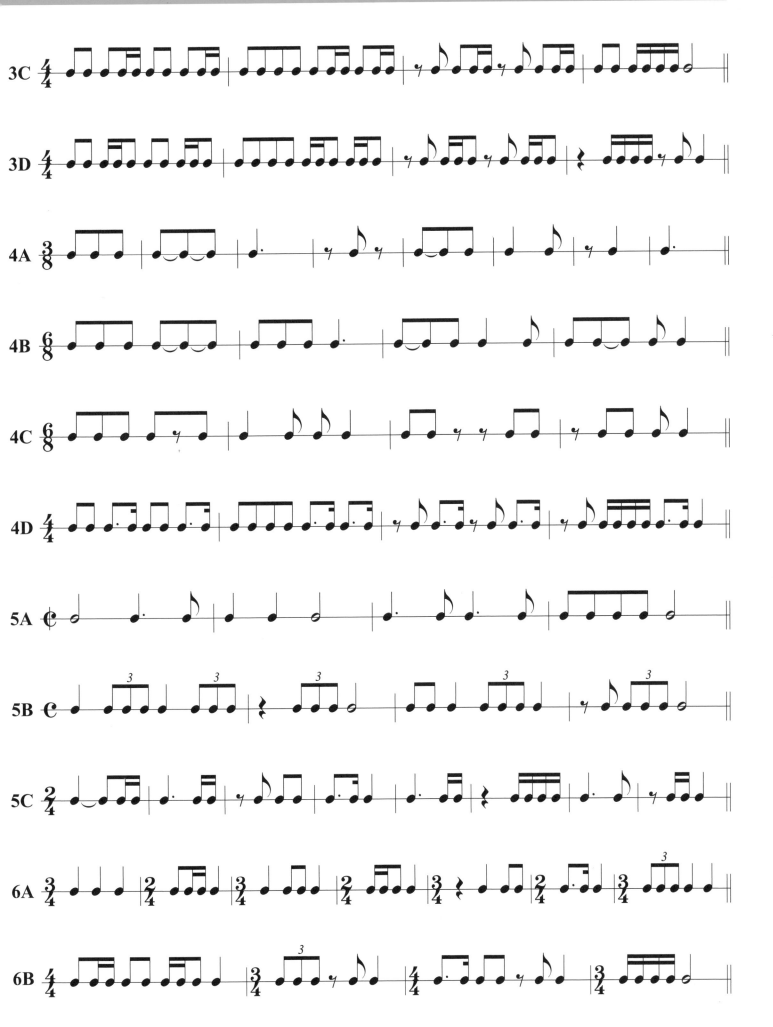

# KEYBOARD PERCUSSION LAYOUT

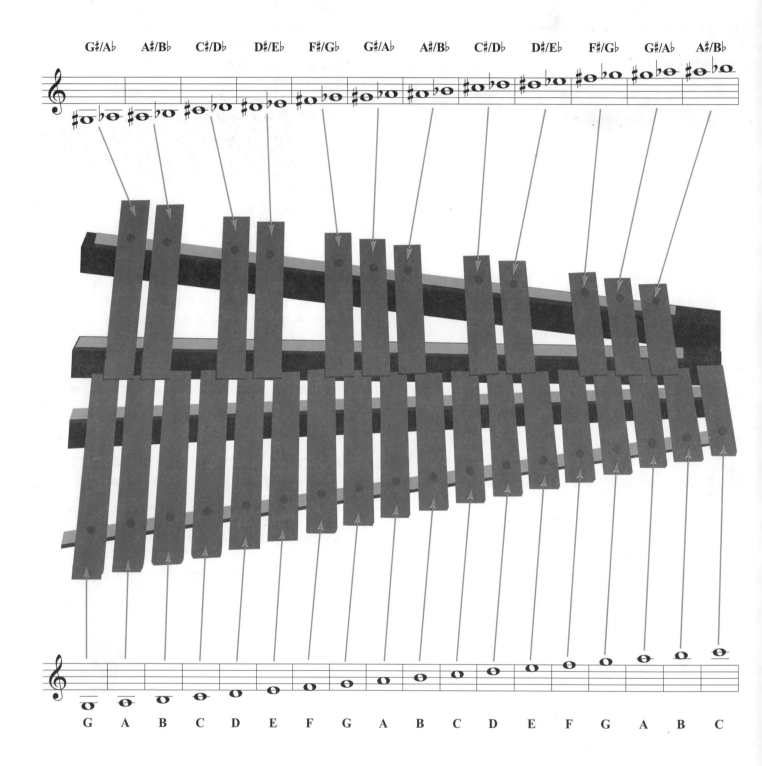

# KEYBOARD PERCUSSION

## BELLS

- Bars – metal alloy or steel
- Mallets – hard rubber, hard plastic or brass
- Sounds 2 octaves higher than written

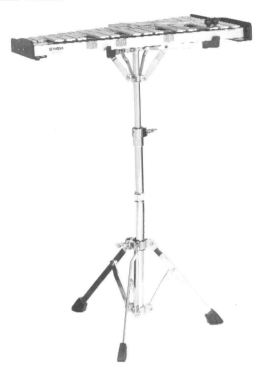

## CHIMES

- Bars – metal tubes
- Mallets – plastic, rawhide or wooden
- Sounding pitch is the same as written pitch

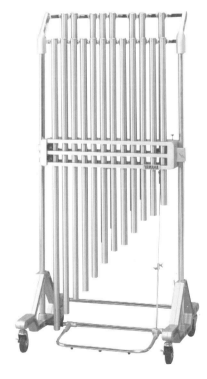

*Photographs courtesy of Yamaha Corporation of America*

## XYLOPHONE

- Bars – wooden or synthetic, with a resonating tube below each bar
- Mallets – hard rubber
- Sounds 1 octave higher than written

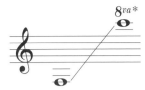

*8va = one octave higher

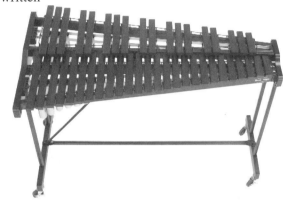

## MARIMBA

- Bars – wooden, wider than xylophone bars, with a resonating tube below each bar
- Mallets – soft to medium yarn covered
- Sounding pitch is the same as written pitch
- Reads bass and treble clefs

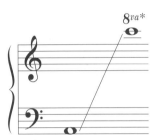

*8va = one octave higher

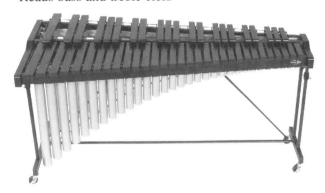

## VIBRAPHONE

- Bars – metal alloy or aluminum, with a resonating tube below each bar
- Mallets – soft to medium cord covered
- Sounding pitch is the same as written pitch

# INDEX

# PERCUSSION INDEX

## TERMS

## SOLOS

### Keyboard Percussion

### Multiple Percussion

### Snare Drum

### Timpani

### Tom-Toms

## ENSEMBLES

## ADDITIONAL STUDIES

# RECOMMENDED STICKS AND MALLETS

- 1 pair of general or 2B snare drum sticks
- 1 pair of hard rubber xylophone mallets
- 1 pair of hard rubber or plastic bell mallets
- 1 pair of general or medium timpani mallets
- 1 pair of medium rubber xylophone mallets (for wood block)
- 1 pair of medium vibraphone mallets (for suspended cymbal)
- 1 pair of medium metal triangle beaters
- 1 medium bass drum mallet
- 1 pair of bass drum roller mallets
- 1 pair of hard felt mallets (for tom-tom)
- 1 pair of thin sticks or timbale sticks (for bongos)
- 1 pair of drum set sticks (5A or 5B)
- 1 pair of medium yarn mallets (for marimba)
- 1 medium gong beater